DEDICATION

To the entrepreneurs inventing new ways to boost college success for first-generation students, people such as Rick Cruz in Houston; Matt Niksch in Chicago; Tammi Sutton in Gaston, North Carolina; Michael Mann in Newark, New Jersey; Phillip Garza in Texas's Rio Grande Valley; Nicole Hurd in Chapel Hill, North Carolina; Pedro Martinez in San Antonio, Texas ... and many more.

THE B.A. BREAKTHROUGH

HOW ENDING DIPLOMA DISPARITIES CAN CHANGE THE FACE OF AMERICA

RICHARD WHITMIRE
FOREWORD BY DANIEL R. PORTERFIELD, PH.D.

TABLE OF CONTENTS

1

2

FOREWORD

BY DANIEL R. PORTERFIELD, PH.D.
President and CEO, The Aspen Institute
Former president, Franklin & Marshall College

— courtesy of Franklin & Marshall College

Today, our world faces a seemingly endless stream of intractable challenges,

from political polarization to generational poverty to climate change. Many are discouraged. In a swiftly changing world, hope may seem in short supply. But that is exactly why this book matters. In *The B.A. Breakthrough,* Richard Whitmire illustrates why building new, and improving existing, educational systems to empower students with college success is needed now – and that it is happening. That's essential to untangling our society's Gordian knots.

Some people will say that we can't afford to invest in young people and education right now – that other problems demand our attention, time, and treasure. But the solutions to all those other problems *require* young people who are educated, empowered, and equipped to act. Their optimism can break the bonds of fatalism and denial.

For the one and the many, education is the key to economic progress and political empowerment. The talent and creativity of our students is America's greatest natural resource – and it is education more than any other investment that will position our country to navigate the enormous workforce transition before us as our once-largest generation, the baby boomers, moves into retirement. Whose work will support the boomers' Medicare and Social Security? Today's schoolchildren. And, so, educating those students well matters profoundly.

We who are older have many worries that keep us up at night. But for so many of our young people, finding solutions is what gets them up in the morning. *The B.A. Breakthrough* gives us the examples and the insights necessary to educate, empower, and equip lower-income students to succeed and to soar.

Whitmire has authored a timely and important book, because he drives home a critical point that matters for students, colleges, and society: that we are learning steadily, and pretty quickly, what works in educating and propelling first-generation students into college opportunity and then sustaining their growth in and through college.

What works is not one single action or game-changing solution, but a set of actions, each of which has been proven demonstrably to make a difference.

We need to expose all low-income students to strong curricula and high-impact teachers in schools that give parents a voice and are accountable for results. We need to provide students with advising and mentoring so that they can envision college and professional pathways that are right for them and successfully navigate the admission process for college and financial aid. We need to work with colleges to increase funding for need-based financial aid, to deepen their recruitment pools of talented students, and to lower the blocks and barriers to college degree attainment that are now well identified – from advising to emergency funds to facilitating belonging. And we need to make sure that government, business, and philanthropy do their parts to invest in results-oriented education at all levels – in particular that they send pro-college, pro-achievement messages to students from underrepresented groups and create a norm and an expectation in society that education is a pathway to economic and political empowerment.

"

The talent and creativity of our students is America's greatest natural resource.

Every reader of this book can find difference-making work to connect to. If one wants to look at pre-college education, the book highlights schools like the KIPP network's public charter schools in Gaston, North Carolina, that are making a difference. If it's college advising and preparation, the book looks at organizations like The Posse Foundation and the College Advising Corps that open doors wide to college opportunity. If the focus is college itself, Whitmire profiles Franklin & Marshall College, where I served as president, and its success in increasing substantially its enrollment of lower-income students through investments in need-based financial aid and strategic partnerships with strong pre-college programs, schools, and leaders.

The book also cites important research from recent years that demonstrates the urgency of the issue. For example, Whitmire points to studies by Stanford University's Caroline Hoxby showing that every year, tens of thousands of high-achieving, low-income students do not apply to a single selective college. And he cites the findings of the Pell Institute that only 11 percent of the lowest-income high school students complete a bachelor's degree in six years.

It's commonplace to say today that the United States is competing in a global knowledge economy where the intellectual power of our citizens will determine both their own life prospects and our economic strength as a nation. It's also often said that every job whose functions can be automated – from tellers to truck drivers – will be. Moreover, we're experiencing profound demographic change with the rapid progress of our youth population to being majority-minority in terms of race and ethnicity and the likelihood of longer life spans because of bold advances in medical technology.

We live in an era of rapidly escalating change. That's undeniable and immutable. Our best answer to the many challenges we face as a country, and the many opportunities we have to improve our standard of living, is to invest boldly, confidently, and determinedly in every stage of the educational process – from preschool to the Ph.D. – with a firm commitment to an ethic of excellence in all we say and do.

Richard Whitmire has documented excellence throughout this book. It's an honest, optimistic, and inspiring read. Let's hope the leaders and approaches he profiles will grow in influence during the next decade and beyond. Our young people deserve nothing less.

INTRODUCTION

This may seem like an odd time to write a book about a "breakthrough" in college success for low-income students.

Generally, the day-to-day news about first-generation students succeeding in college is grim: The 2018 National Assessment of Educational Progress report showed little overall improvement in the K-12 years that would predict better academic outcomes for these students and, worse, the gaps between the low and high achievers are only growing wider.[1] In October 2018, the new ACT scores revealed the same: Except for Asian students, college readiness is slipping.[2] Although record numbers of first-generation students now enter college, few end up earning degrees. According to the Pell Institute, 11 percent of students from families in the lowest-income quartile earn bachelor's degrees within six years, compared with 58 percent of the students who grow up in the highest-income group.[3] There are now more college dropouts than high school dropouts.[4]

There are many other ways to measure these astonishing college success gaps, including along racial and ethnic lines. I'll review the data in Chapter 2, but just to offer a quick preview: The numbers shift slightly, back and forth, depending on whether you measure family wealth versus family income, black and Hispanic students versus low-income families.[5] But in the end, everything pretty much looks just as dismal as the Pell numbers, often worse.

On the surface, therefore, declaring there's a breakthrough in college success for first-generation college students appears to be a prediction that ranges somewhere between naively optimistic and rash. But the promising news about college completion is findable, if you know where to look. That's what this book is about. Knowing where to look leads to knowing how to build on and scale the emerging breakthrough.

START WITH THE PERSONAL SUCCESS STORIES, AND BUILD FROM THERE

It was at the end of a phone conversation with Ashley Copeland, who was raised by a single mother in a trailer in rural North Carolina, when she said something that was both innocent and revealing. "You know, I wouldn't be talking to you if not for them."

The "them" are the co-founders of the KIPP Gaston charter schools, Tammi Sutton and Caleb Dolan, Teach for America teachers who decided to stay in tiny Gaston, North Carolina, and found their own public charter schools. It was those schools, which Copeland entered as a fifth-grader, that sharply altered her life trajectory, leading to graduation from

Duke University, a good job in Washington, D.C., and owning two properties in expensive Washington with plans to buy more.

She was right, of course. Had she stayed in her struggling local school there, the odds of her graduating from Duke would have been astronomically long. She might be living somewhere in rural North Carolina, and I wouldn't be interviewing her.

It would be easy to write off Copeland's story as a first-rate, feel-good anecdote. Poor black girl from rural North Carolina beats the odds. My research suggests otherwise. In recent years, I've been following a paradigm shift in college success rates for low-income, minority students. This shift is being driven by three underappreciated but very powerful factors playing out side by side. First, there's a growing number of colleges that have stepped forward to accept responsibility for not just admitting these students but ensuring they succeed. Second, there's a surge in tightly targeted funding from advocacy groups, nonprofits, and philanthropies that focus on smarter college counseling. They sense a win here and know exactly where to place their money to make an impact.

Finally, there's the surprise factor that's at the heart of *The B.A. Breakthrough*: Some high schools, most of them belonging to high-performing charter networks, have figured out how to prepare first-generation students to not just enter college, but then track them through college to make sure they actually earn a degree. This is an unexpected development, a paradigm shift and the reason why the breakthrough still hovers below the public awareness radar. Higher education experts tend to know relatively little about these public charter networks, and most traditional school districts resent their existence and deliberately ignore their lessons learned.

To be clear, public charter schools are controversial and not always better than their counterparts in the traditional education world. And there's no disputing that the fired-up progressive left has turned against them, in part because of their embrace by President Donald Trump. But their being controversial and politically complicated should not prevent us from dispassionately evaluating their academic records with respect to college success. This requires "full stop" thinking that, unfortunately, not everyone caught up in the bitter education policy wars is capable of. The top charter networks truly have come up with something unique here. But there's a catch: What they discovered will never have a broad impact unless the far larger traditional school districts adopt those same practices. Until recently, that seemed unlikely, but there's encouraging evidence of those barriers coming down.

The B.A. Breakthrough has a trajectory. It started less than a decade ago when researchers started studying low-income, high-performing students – the roughly 60,300 students each year who score in the top quarter of students in math and reading at the beginning of high school.[6] I've heard them referred to as the "Hoxby kids," named for Caroline Hoxby, the Stanford University researcher who was one of the first to surface this group in 2012 and ask why they got educationally cheated. Why do a quarter of them never even apply to college? Why were so few landing at top colleges?[7] Foundations and universities stepped in to begin correcting that problem, with the American Talent Initiative bringing together top universities to address an obvious inequity by admitting more low-income, high-achieving students. The message appears to be getting through: In September 2018, U.S. News & World Report announced it was changing its college ratings formula to reward colleges that support the success of their low-income students.[8] The announcement came a year after a Politico piece outlined how the rankings encourage colleges to do less, not more, to help first-generation students.[9] Even more interesting: Three months later, six Democratic senators, including two presidential contenders, released a statement saying the publication didn't go far enough. The rankings need even more revisions to reverse the damage, they contended.

A move to improve college graduation rates among low-income, minority students also unfolded among the non-elite colleges, starting with innovations such as "corequisite remediation," in which new college students needing remediation get green-lighted to take for-credit classes while also receiving side-by-side remedial help. That one reform alone helped thousands of students stay on track to earn degrees. Institutions such as Georgia State University pioneered early warning systems to detect students in trouble and correct problems quickly, and also created Pounce, personalized text messaging to keep students on track, more broadly known as the "nudge." Community colleges, long considered black holes of higher education and yet a key entry point for many first-generation students, improved guidance with programs such as Pathways that keep students on a tight track to achieve their goals. Getting community college presidents on board with college success reforms became the goal of the Aspen Presidential Fellowship for Community College Excellence, established in 2016, one of many innovations from The Aspen Institute, a nonpartisan education and policy studies organization, which has become a national leader in the college success movement.

Less noticed in this trajectory timeline was the parallel push by the big charter networks to ensure that all their students, not just the most talented, won spots in college and went on to earn degrees – a very different goal from seeking spots in top colleges for low-income, high-performing students. What the charter networks were doing is best described as "democratizing" higher education. In Chapter 3, I'll show how that's happening in the most unlikely of places.

There are reasons to believe that the breakthrough will build, in part because at this point there's only early coordination between these three driving forces. When does all this reach a tipping point? We will recognize the tipping points when traditional school districts, which now pay little or no attention to the fates of their alumni, start tracking them through college and reporting the results to parents. (Actually, that's beginning to happen already, on a very small scale.)

We'll see a tipping point when hundreds of colleges, not just a limited network, adopt college success practices that support first-generation students. (That's happening already at a significant number of colleges.) One factor motivating colleges: they are running out of students, so retaining the ones they have, including more at-risk students from low-income families, suddenly becomes a must.[10] A second factor motivating colleges: the $16.5 billion they lose each year in tuition from students who drop out. The irony: the more colleges get disrupted by demographics, the more attention they need to pay to low-income students.[11]

And finally, we'll know a tipping point when students, even those in the highest-poverty high schools, get college advising that steers them into colleges that will lead to diplomas and away from colleges that become debt-generating dead ends. (Also happening quickly.) Smart guidance counseling for students amounts to low-hanging fruit;

it doesn't take rocket science to determine which colleges have default rates that are higher than their graduation rates. Just pay attention to The Education Trust's College Results website, which ranks each college based on successful completions, for all students.

It's hard to overstate the potential impact here. Consider just one of three factors, the high-performing charter networks that focus on college completion. At high schools run by well-known networks such as Uncommon Schools and YES Prep, approximately half of their alumni (nearly all low-income, minority students) earn bachelor's degrees within six years. Among Ashley Copeland's founding Class of 2009 at KIPP Gaston in North Carolina, 61 percent earned bachelor's degrees within six years. A reminder: The national rate for low-income minority students is about 11 percent. There are a lot of things that charter schools don't do that well, but college success is not one of them. At Uncommon Schools, the software program that tracks the progress of their alumni through college predicts that within six years, 70 percent of Uncommon graduates will earn a bachelor's degree. That exceeds by several points the national college graduation rate for well-off students.

The scale for charter schools is admittedly modest. But consider the possibilities. Earning a college degree remains the best way for students who grew up in poverty to achieve economic mobility and reverse their fortunes.[12] If these college success strategies can spread to traditional public schools and districts, it is logical to suggest that what's happening here could develop into the most effective anti-poverty program ever launched in this country – if, and this is a big if, traditional districts follow suit. And what the charter networks have accomplished with college success is just part of *The B.A. Breakthrough* story.

There's little disagreement that the growing equity gap is America's biggest Achilles' heel.[13] For more than a decade, Americans have watched the daily headlines about the rich getting richer and the poor failing to dig their way out – much of it connected directly to educational opportunity, or lack of it. Most would agree this violates a fundamental notion of what this country represents, starting with fairness. This breakthrough may be a beginning to reversing the widening of that gap.

THE BOOK'S ORIGINS

It was the charter networks that first led me to this issue. For most of the roughly 25 years I've been writing about education, my focus was on traditional urban districts. Who among them qualified as pioneers in educating low-income students? But it seemed like every time I declared a particular district a maybe-winner, the backsliding began, often because a pioneering superintendent got pushed aside by opponents upset with the reforms. (I truly hope Long Beach, California, a district that under the leadership of Superintendent Christopher Steinhauser has shown what's possible, especially with low-income students, persists as a national exception to the rule.) That's mostly why Los Angeles-based philanthropist Eli Broad famously walked away from his much-acclaimed "Broad Prize" for the traditional districts making the most progress with disadvantaged students (Full disclosure: I was once part of a Broad Prize team that visited all the finalist districts). Backsliding.

The trials of turning around a historically awful urban district, a district such as Washington, D.C., became painfully obvious during the year I spent following former D.C. chancellor Michelle Rhee for the book *The Bee Eater*. For a moment, set aside whether you agree or disagree with Rhee's in-your-face reforms. What's sobering, and sad, is that prior to Rhee's arrival her many (future) critics were perfectly content to allow D.C. schools to fail thousands of families. What got them all fired up, marching in the streets and calling for her head, was the prospect of real change that shook up the status quo they preferred. Today, D.C. schools are doing better, but progress is slow.

After that experience I decided to give charter schools a try. Was there any hope there? Who among them were the pioneers? At times, that search proved to be almost as frustrating as examining traditional districts. When looking only at measures such as test scores, the truth was difficult to sort out. Are they really doing better? And charter schools experience their own brand of turbulence, as I discovered while spending a year following the expansion of California-based Rocketship schools for the book *On the Rocketship*. Although Rocketship schools do some great work today in California, Milwaukee, and Washington, D.C., the original dreams of their co-founders, to level the nation's achievement gaps all on their own, fizzled.

Only recently did I start examining the core promise charter school leaders from day one made to parents: We will help your children win college degrees, degrees that are unlikely to materialize should you leave your children in your beleaguered neighborhood schools. Given that many charter networks launched with elementary schools, and college success is measured six years after graduating from high school, only in the past couple of years has evaluating this promise been possible.

What I'm finding is exciting. Yes, there were plenty of missed goals and missteps trying to make that promise a reality, but the ultimate results in recent years are promising, maybe even extraordinary. In the big nonprofit charter networks I examined, where the graduates were nearly all low-income students of color, the success rate of earning a bachelor's degree at the six-year mark was at least double the rate for comparable students not in these networks. A few outliers were doing four or even five times better, depending on the metric used. All that was laid out in a 2017 series I wrote for The 74, called The Alumni.

But *The B.A. Breakthrough* is not just about charters. While planning to turn The Alumni series into a book with a focus on storytelling through the eyes of those charter school alumni, I realized that while a lot of groundbreaking work on college completion emerged from the charters, there was far more to this story. That's why you'll find stories about the other forces driving change for first-generation students, including college success programs at traditional districts such as Houston Independent School District, organizations such as the Posse Foundation, which ensures that first-generation college-goers have familiar friends to turn to – their posse – and scores of colleges that, individually, are creating their own breakthroughs.

The B.A. Breakthrough is, of course, more about people than programs. It's about those KIPP Gaston alumni in the founding Class of 2009. Throughout the book, I track those young men and women, now in their late 20s, and follow-on classes at Gaston. Near the end, I describe a party overlooking the U.S. Capitol where alumni gathered to plan their 10th reunion party and exchange stories. Their lives have changed; their friendships have not. Had Caleb Dolan and Tammi Sutton not landed in Gaston as Teach for America rookies and then decided to dig in with their own school, odds are few of them would have become professionals.

As I take readers through the developments that make up *The B.A. Breakthrough,* I'll keep a running narrative on the Gaston alumni and how they became college graduates. What happened in Gaston is a little-known story that everyone needs to hear about – and an insight into how the breakthrough can push through to its tipping point.

Author's notes:

1. There's no single term that encompasses the group of students I'm writing about. A first-generation college-goer isn't necessarily low-income or minority. In my family, I'm a first-generation college graduate. My target group: low-income students, most of them students of color, who are almost always first-generation, and who struggle to earn college degrees. When I use the term first-generation, that's the group I intend to describe. To put it simply, students who are one car repair away from dropping out of college.

2. Throughout the book I'll measure college success mostly by bachelor's degrees earned at the six-year mark. That's for expediency, not to downgrade the importance of associate's degrees and certificates.

1

THE
BREAKTHROUGH

IN GASTON, NORTH CAROLINA WHERE B.A. DEGREES DOUBLED

KIPP Gaston co-founder Tammi Sutton in 2006 with students, including
some members of the founding class of 2009, who were starting 10th grade.
— *courtesy of KIPP Gaston*

CHAPTER 1

On the short drive from Interstate 95 into Gaston, North Carolina,

a one-stoplight home to a little over 1,000 folks, you can see a paper mill smokestack belching on the horizon. "Smells like money" – that's what they say in every paper mill town. You don't see any of the nearby prisons, but working as a corrections officer is a common job here. Plus peanut farming. Or soybeans.

This is rural North Carolina. Not like trendy, upscale Smoky Mountains kind of rural, where the hillsides just below the national park get dotted at night with the dusk-to-dawn lights of million-dollar-plus homes. This is the poor, flatland kind of rural poverty, nearly invisible off I-95. The kind of rural where, despite the young people here being next to the East Coast's most prominent traffic corridor, most of what they know about the outside world comes from watching TV. If white folks have even heard of Gaston, it's probably because of Lake Gaston, a dammed-up hydroelectric reservoir well out of town that's a magnet for well-off retirees. That Gaston doesn't mix much with this Gaston.

As might be predicted, the percent of residents here in Northampton County with college degrees has typically been one of the lowest in the state. But recently, the percentage of county residents with full four-year college degrees – B.A.s, not just two-year degrees – has been rising fast. A doubling in the past five years. How can that happen? Explaining that phenomenon leads to a good story, a story connected to a school in Gaston built on 27 acres of scraped-off peanut and soybean red clay fields: KIPP Gaston College Prep – home of "The Pride."

THE DUO WHO WOULD STOP AT NOTHING TO START A SCHOOL

Perhaps the best place to begin is in the spring of 1999, when Teach for America founder Wendy Kopp, pregnant with her first child, decided to take time off to visit high-performing TFA teachers, visits she describes in her first book, *One Day, All Children*....[1]

A priority stop for her was Gaston, where she had heard about the stunning success experienced at Gaston Middle School by TFA teachers Tammi Sutton and Caleb Dolan. Kopp flew into Raleigh, rented a car, drove to Gaston, and discovered a tiny town that, she writes, could serve as a Hollywood set for a "lost in time" movie.

At Gaston Middle School, nearly all the students were both black and poor. There, four TFA teachers constituted a third of the faculty members teaching core subjects. And they were having a huge impact. Three years before Kopp arrived, Gaston Middle was one of the lowest-performing schools in the state, with fewer than half the students at grade level. But now, with the jolt felt from the TFA teachers, the school had achieved an "exemplary" ranking in the state's accountability system – standardized scores, on average, rose by 30 percentage points– and the principal, Lucy Edwards, had been named the county's principal of the year two years in a row.

One teacher in particular, Tammi Sutton, caught Kopp's eye, and Kopp settled in to watch her teach. "I walked into Tammi's classroom to be greeted by a 5-foot-5-inch woman with short sandy hair, a determined manner, and rich southern accent," writes Kopp in her book. Kopp watched Sutton and her students dissect poems. Recalls Sutton: "We were discussing a poem that I had written – lessons learned from my 25 years, and the kids would write the same about their 13 years. The poem was semi-personal, which made things a bit awkward. Here was Wendy Kopp sitting in the classroom listening."

That evening, Sutton and Dolan drove Kopp through the region to show her where their students lived, some of their houses located down dirt paths. It was an insight into rural poverty. Later, they talked over a chicken tenders dinner at the Texas Steakhouse, at the time the fanciest restaurant in the region. Eventually, Kopp pieced together the strategy behind Sutton's and Dolan's success, a strategy that went far beyond academics. "She [Sutton] got to know them through church dinners, cookouts, and family trips where she was invited along. She started a Saturday night basketball league. She and another corps member planned an extracurricular trip to Egypt; even though she and her kids only got as far as Orlando, the trip was a bonding experience," writes Kopp.

The traditional academic day wasn't enough to catch up her students, Sutton concluded, so she convinced corps members to volunteer their Saturday mornings to host tutoring sessions. Plus, Sutton and other corps members persuaded the principal to lengthen the school day by 45 minutes. Finally, they worked out an arrangement with the principal and families to keep the students in the classroom until 7 p.m. working on homework.

A special goal for Sutton was improving her students' writing, one of their biggest academic weaknesses, according to state tests. Kopp writes: "By the end of the year, Tammi had met the goal by her own assessment as well as the state's: 96 percent of her sixty students performed above state standards for acceptable writing, and many of them performed well above those standards."

In her book, Kopp focuses on Sutton, but her partner in achieving these results was Dolan. Sutton and Dolan are two very different people from very different parts of the country who happened to draw the same TFA assignment. Born in Mount Holly, New Jersey, Sutton grew up in a military family that moved a lot. Her parents divorced when she was in middle school, and for most of her life she was raised by her mother. What she mentions first about her mother is that she grew up in a small town in Michigan and yet still managed to land a National Merit Scholarship award, which she planned to use at Michigan State University. But that lasted only a semester; she dropped out to marry her high school sweetheart and, in Sutton's words, "begin 20 years of a less than empowering marriage." That thwarted ambition is something that continues to haunt Sutton, and it affects how she feels about her students in Gaston. No opportunity should be lost.

Sutton was living in North Carolina when she graduated from high school, and she could tell the schools there, both high schools and colleges, were deeply segregated. That was very different from living in integrated military communities – "utopian bubbles," as she puts it. So in choosing colleges she looked for the most diverse ones available, which is why she settled on the University of North Carolina at Greensboro. There, she studied English and political science with the goal of going to law school – but not before signing up with Teach for America, which assigned her to Gaston.

Dolan grew up in rural Maine and entered Maine's Colby College, where he studied creative writing and philosophy. Drawn by the promise of a chance to make "meaningful change," Dolan signed up for a TFA interview. "TFA had no standards back then," said Dolan, a master of self-deprecating humor. "I went to the interview in hiking boots and hippie gear and they still took me." He asked to go to New York City, but instead got assigned to Gaston.

Finding themselves in the same small middle school, Sutton and Dolan at first had very different experiences. Sutton, self-described as an indifferent student in both high school and college, quickly found her calling, a born teacher who all her life had been searching out a social justice cause. "Tammi was the most naturally talented teacher I've still ever met," said Dolan. "She was really good from the beginning and I was really bad."

Sutton taught seventh-grade reading and writing, and Dolan got assigned the kids who had failed the state reading test the year before. "They had me rather than PE, so it was a really desirable class," said Dolan, tongue firmly in cheek. "These kids, wonderful kids, for probably good reason ignored me. They would sigh and roll their eyes when they walked into my class. And then they would walk over to Tammi's class for the next period, greet her at the door and smile and laugh. I was just like, 'What the hell am I doing wrong? What is she doing that when she talks, kids listen?' She would be firm but also warm. So I started paying attention to what she was doing."

Dolan began investing more personal time in his students. Students who failed tests got invited to stay after school for extra tutoring and homework help. Often, that got followed up by some basketball and a ride home, with a stop at Hardee's for some burgers. Dolan, who today oversees KIPP's Massachusetts schools, did things in Gaston he'd never advise his teachers to do today in Boston – they're just not sustainable or advisable at scale. But back then, in tiny Gaston, it was doable, and it worked, with both Dolan and Sutton getting to know their students and their families. "It was crazy and sleepless, but we really spent a lot of time with the kids. It was pretty neat." That strong school culture they nurtured would form the bedrock for what would become KIPP Gaston.

For Sutton, arriving at Gaston Middle appeared to be an awakening. This job, teaching students in a tiny, impoverished town, students who without fierce interventions would have limited college options, quickly became a calling. These students would not miss the chance her mother once had at Michigan State University. Nor would they become indifferent students as she once was in high school and college. Not if Tammi Sutton had anything to say about it.

Quickly, Sutton and Dolan became known as the duo who would stop at nothing. In their second year, they decided to take their students on a field trip to the University of North Carolina at Chapel Hill. "We had been hyping this trip," said Dolan, "telling them this was going to be a really big thing, and they had earned it." The morning of the trip, the 30 students showed up, but the bus was locked in the bus yard. "Tammi was always very good at convincing me to do ridiculous things, so we cut the bolts on the bus yard and seized the bus." That created quite a buzz, which only got louder when the students, who loved the trip, talked it up big when they returned. The bottom line to the buzz: There's something more to this life here at Gaston Middle School than just test scores, something more than just going to class.

It was infectious, with other teachers joining in with special events. Groups who did all their homework got to go to the state fair. Sutton and Dolan were creating a reputation. "All of a sudden, kids are doing well on state tests, they're visiting colleges, they're talking about different topics. I think that got parents excited. They believed in us," said Sutton.

Those trips, to colleges and elsewhere, helped break down the social isolation they saw in their students. "I remember kids writing that their dream home was a double-wide trailer. That blew my mind.

> *All of a sudden, kids are doing well on state tests, they're visiting colleges, they're talking about different topics. I think that got parents excited. They believed in us.*

Or they might write that one day they hoped to visit Rocky Mount, which is 30 miles away down 95," said Sutton.

By the time Wendy Kopp showed up at Gaston Middle School, both Sutton and Dolan had completed their two-year TFA obligations and opted to stay on as teachers. This was their third year teaching. At the time, Kopp's appearance amounted to an interesting and flattering visit by an education celebrity – and nothing more. But her visit ended up changing both their lives. After seeing Sutton and Dolan in action, she recognized their leadership potential and recalls telling them during that chicken tenders dinner, "You know, you two should start a school."

What's not in Kopp's book is what happened after that. Kopp knew both KIPP founders, Dave Levin and Mike Feinberg. As part of her book research, she had spent a week in Levin's classroom in New York City. Not long after her return from Gaston, Kopp recalls standing in her kitchen in New York City having a phone conversation with Feinberg, who was looking to expand KIPP regions.

"By the way," she told him, "I just met two people who need to start a school. These guys are the real deal." Kopp's recommendation was all Feinberg needed to know. He called Sutton and Dolan and left a message for them to call back. Feinberg's call went unanswered for at least three days. Both were too busy teaching and coaching basketball and track. When they finally connected, Feinberg flew them to Houston and offered an amazing opportunity: KIPP has fresh expansion money, he told them. The network would arrange training as Fisher Fellows, where new school leaders are trained, and then give them each their own new regions – Tammi to Atlanta, Dolan to Denver.

The offer was tempting, especially to Dolan. "For me, I hadn't been on a date since college at that point, so I was like, 'Oh my God. Wow. Denver sounds great.'" Sutton was tempted as well. "For about 24 or 48 hours, it was really exciting. At the time, we were making maybe $23,000, and they were offering a Fisher Fellowship, which would more than double our salaries. We were both single. We hadn't had bagels in a very long time. I had friends in Atlanta. All that seemed super exciting. But at the end of the day, I couldn't imagine walking into my seventh-grade classroom and telling them I was leaving. That was it."

Dolan came to the same conclusion. Tempting, but he just couldn't leave. But instead of turning down Feinberg, they made a counteroffer: We'll start a new KIPP region, but only if we can do it here in Gaston. What our middle school students desperately need, they told Feinberg, is a challenging and caring high school to attend after they leave here.

Feinberg was skeptical. How would you convince great teachers to come to Gaston? Where would you find an effective board to oversee the school? Where would you find a building? Plus, KIPP at the time specialized in middle schools, not high schools. But Sutton and Dolan pushed back: All the reasons you just cited as to why it won't work in Gaston are exactly the reasons you should do this. Prove you can truly be a national model, even in rural areas. Let this be your first rural site.

Feinberg agreed, creating a first-of-its-kind KIPP school. KIPP Gaston College Prep, better known as KIPP GCP, home of The Pride.

A LEAP OF FAITH AND KIPP GASTON IS LAUNCHED

Sutton chose to keep teaching at Gaston Middle School while Dolan went through a year of leadership training as a Fisher Fellow, a fellowship Sutton would opt for later. Then it was time to recruit students for their new school. The first students were easy to find – the middle schoolers they already taught who came from parents who already knew them. But after that, recruiting became more difficult. Place yourself in the positions of Sutton and Dolan: You're promoting the KIPP brand, which nobody's heard of. You haven't hired any teachers. You're championing a charter school at a time when nobody in Gaston even knew what that was. And, worst of all, you have no actual school building.

Most challenging: You're white, recruiting in low-income, rural black neighborhoods, saying, "Trust us; we're here to do right by your children."

Working in their favor, said Dolan, was a factor he dubs "the power of cousins." In Gaston, every student they recruited could point to scores of cousins who might also be interested. Often, those cousins lived in the same trailer park. "The power of cousins in Gaston is immeasurable," said Dolan, "because ultimately that's, like, everybody. Everybody is a couple of degrees away. I went to a few churches where people were kind enough to let me talk for a minute. I think they recognized early on that I was a sinner but were still kind enough to let me come in."

Also working in their favor was Southern hospitality. Most families were at least willing to listen. "At some moment in the conversation there was this moment where you could tell they were thinking, 'Why the hell should I believe you? People like you have not necessarily done well by me in the past.'" But the families, Dolan said, could tell that he and Sutton were true believers in their cause. It came through. Thus, one line often worked: "If you come to Gaston College Prep, you're going to work hard, you're going to have a lot of fun, you're going to graduate from college – and you're going to help your mother retire." That last line, Dolan said, always got a laugh.

The closing line, though, was usually the clincher: "I'm the principal of the new school, and here's my phone number." What local school leader had ever visited their home and offered their personal phone number?

To this day, Dolan marvels at the trust the parents put in them. "I mean, I was 26 at the time, barely able to tie a tie." Why did they commit? "I think people just so desperately wanted something better that they were able to make leaps of faith. They recognized the difference between their current situation and what's possible. If your child is unhappy in school, bored, failing or whatever, they saw that there just might be something different. That's why they trusted us."

SIX YEARS OUT, A 61% COLLEGE GRADUATION RATE

KIPP Gaston first opened as a middle school in 2001 with 80 students. Their school site: the 27 acres of former peanut and soybean fields returned to red clay to make room for four modular trailers.

Their transportation: three used school buses painted blue. KIPP Pride High opened in 2005, with its founding class, the Pride of 2009. There were 71 students in that very first class.

Early on, Sutton and Dolan selected The Pride as the school motto. Unlike other KIPP schools, where students are known as KIPPsters, here in Gaston they are members of The Pride. "It's the dual meaning that attracted us," said Sutton, "a sense of a family of lions coming together from different communities, a collective group that cares about both individual and group success."

One of their first hires to teach fifth-grade math was Carolyn B. Bell, whose twin daughters, Gara and Cara, had been taught by Sutton and Dolan for two years at Gaston Middle School. Bell, who was then a teacher at a local elementary school, knew she was witnessing something special going on with her daughters. "Wow, they were just excellent teachers. Around here, we don't have a lot of good teachers, teachers who aren't there just for the paycheck." Her daughters were too old to join the new KIPP school, but she wanted to be part of it, so she switched to teach there.

The KIPP school drew in the same kinds of students she had been teaching, but produced very different outcomes, she said. Bell credits the two years of exposure to Sutton and Dolan for how her daughters turned out, both college graduates and successful professionals. (One is a speech pathologist, the other an assistant principal for a KIPP school in Durham.)

In 2009, 48 seniors, The Pride of 2009, walked across the stage to receive diplomas. At the six-year mark, where college success is measured, 61 percent of them had earned college degrees (all but two of them four-year degrees). The most current figure, at the eight-year mark, is 63 percent having earned degrees. That number may not sound extraordinary, but it is. Nationally, only 11 percent of children raised in the lowest-income quartile earn bachelor's degrees within six years. And that may be understating the gap. The KIPP families in Gaston would fall toward the bottom of that lowest-income quartile, and that class was almost entirely African American, which undoubtedly would push the college graduation odds even longer.

> " At the six-year mark, where college success is measured, 61 percent of them had earned college degrees.

Statistically speaking, a class of 48 students means nothing, right? And didn't the founding class get special attention? Compared with the next graduating class, where the degree-earning rate was a more modest 48 percent, it would appear so. But the Class of 2011 was back up to 61.5 percent at the six-year mark. What about the small numbers? A cautionary note, for sure. But the numbers of KIPP Gaston alumni are growing each year.

So far, 568 Pride graduates have become alumni. Each class has seen 100 percent acceptance to four-year universities, and each class has attracted more than $1 million in scholarships. Something compelling is going on in this one-stoplight town. What can possibly explain the recent surge in residents with four-year degrees residing there, other than KIPP Gaston graduates who return and teachers arriving to teach at the growing KIPP network?

In Northampton County, home to Gaston, the percentage of residents holding bachelor's degrees doubled over the past five years, according to Census data. According to state education data, only 20 percent of Northampton County students scored 17 or better on the ACT. Among KIPP Gaston students, 79 percent did as well or better. No sophisticated industries have opened up in the county over the past five years. The paper mills and prisons didn't create that boost in college degrees. There's only one remaining source: KIPP Gaston.

True, a mere 568 alumni is an iffy indicator. And in the national economic picture, Northampton County is a flyspeck. Perhaps, but the Gaston network is growing. Today, KIPP Gaston has three schools serving 1,244 students. Its KIPP region has six schools serving 1,914 students in Gaston, Halifax, and Durham. Still small, but when viewed in a far larger context of KIPP nationally and the other big successful charter networks, a pattern emerges – a pattern that says something about the beginnings of a breakthrough.

THE PROBLEM IS NOT COLLEGE ATTENDANCE, IT'S COLLEGE COMPLETION

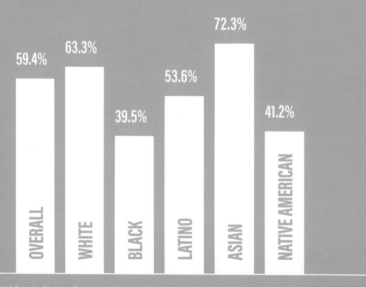

Figure 2: Racial Gaps in Six-Year Graduation Rates at Four-Year Institutions, 2015

— Source: National Center for Education Statistics. 2016 Digest for Education Statistics. Table 326.10

CHAPTER 2

America's higher education problem is not a college enrollment problem.

The percentage of students who head straight to college after high school has risen from 63 percent in 2000 to 70 percent in 2016, according to the Department of Education.[1] What we have is a graduation problem, especially among low-income minority students: Just 11 percent of students from the lowest-income quartile earn bachelor's degrees within six years (the commonly used indicator of college success), compared with 58 percent of students who come from the highest-income group, according to the Pell Institute.[2]

The National Center for Education Statistics tracked a 2002 cohort of U.S. students, finding that only 14.6 percent of those whose families are in the lowest- income quartile earned bachelor's degrees within 10 years, compared with 46 percent from the highest-income group.

The astonishingly low college success rates alarm many liberal-leaning groups, such as the Education Trust, but also worry conservatives, who note that the problem is not limited to low-income students. Rick Hess, director of education policy studies at the right-leaning American Enterprise Institute, led a team that examined the dilemma.[3] Writes Hess: "In 2016, more than 40 percent of all students who started at a four-year college six years earlier had not earned a degree ... This means that nearly two million students who begin college each year will drop out before earning a diploma ... There are more than 600 four-year colleges where less than a third of students will graduate within six years of arriving on campus."

But the issue is most acute among blacks and Hispanics, where the college enrollment rates keep rising but the success rates – those who actually walk away with four-year degrees – are barely better than flat.[4] They drop out before earning degrees. The overall college graduation figures reveal the imbalance. Just 14 percent of black adults and 11 percent of Hispanic adults hold bachelor's degrees, compared with 24 percent of whites.

Overall, about a third of the students who enroll in college still haven't earned a bachelor's degree at the six-year mark, according to the National Student Clearinghouse.[5] Not surprisingly, the dropout rates are higher for first-generation students. A third of first-generation students drop out of college at the three-year mark, compared with a quarter of students whose parents have degrees, according to the National Center for Education Statistics.

Various government agencies and advocacy organizations have different ways of cutting and framing the data, so the rates are going to appear slightly different, depending on the report. But one thing never changes: the significant completion gaps by race and income.

Among Hispanics ages 25-34, just 17.8 percent have a bachelor's degree, compared with 43.7 percent of young white adults.[6] Roughly half of Hispanic students who start at four-year colleges as first-time, full-time students earn a bachelor's degree from those institutions, a rate 10 percentage points below whites.

> "
> *Just 14 percent of black adults and 11 percent of Hispanic adults hold bachelor's degrees, compared with 24 percent of whites.*

For black students, the college success gaps are even starker.[7] Forty-one percent who enrolled in four-year colleges as first-time, full-time students earned degrees there, which is 22 percentage points below white students. Especially troubling is the lack of intergenerational improvement among black adults.[8] Only 30 percent of younger blacks, ages 25-34, have earned a degree, compared with 27 percent of older black adults, ages 55-64. Now compare that to whites, among whom young adults today earn college degrees at a rate 10 percentage points higher than older whites.

FOR BLACK AND HISPANIC COLLEGE STUDENTS, WHERE YOU GO MATTERS MOST

Although colleges and universities have been improving their overall graduation rates, that doesn't mean all students are benefiting. Among colleges that improved their graduation rates from 2003 to 2013, more than half didn't make the same gains for their black students, according to the Education Trust.[9] More ominously, at about a third of the colleges and universities in that study, the graduation rates for black students either flattened or declined. The states with the highest degree attainment for black students: Georgia, Maryland, Nebraska, New Mexico, and Virginia. The lowest: Louisiana, Michigan, Missouri, Nevada, Oklahoma, and Wisconsin.

We know that both black and Hispanic students take the most remediation courses in college, which greatly increases their odds of dropping out.[10] For poor students, no-credit classes that cost money are non-starters. About 70 percent of black community college students end up in remedial courses, and almost half of those enrolled at non-flagship four-year institutions do. Many of those students have to take remedial courses in both English and math. Concludes Complete College America: "Forty percent of African American students and 30 percent of Latino students and 32 percent of Pell students at community colleges are enrolled in both remedial math and English. As a result, these students have, at a minimum, two additional courses they must enroll in, complete and pay for as part of their postsecondary education ... It is easy to understand how placement in remedial education could negatively impact efforts to boost completion rates among students of color and low-income students."

Here's one certainty we know about Hispanic and black students: where they enroll in college makes the biggest difference. The Education Trust, which documents college success differences as part of its CollegeResults.org tracker, offers this example: At Whittier College in California, Hispanic students graduate at a rate 5.5 percentage points higher than white students. By comparison, at Mercy College in New York, white students graduate at a rate that is 22 percentage points higher than Hispanics.

For black students, the lesson is similar: Where you go matters most. The Education Trust offers this example: At the University of California, Riverside, 67 percent of black students earn bachelor's degrees within six years, compared with 44 percent at the University of Illinois at Chicago. At Middle Tennessee State University, the black graduation rate is 40 percent, compared with 20 percent at Eastern Michigan University. At California State University, Fullerton, the black graduation rate is 56 percent, compared with a rate of 39 percent at the University of Texas at San Antonio.

Nationally, the graduation rate for Pell students – low-income students qualifying for federal grants – is 51 percent, compared with 65 percent for non-Pell students. When the Education Trust scrubbed the numbers for 1,100 public and private institutions, it found something compelling: Half of that graduation gap can be explained by Pell students enrolling in institutions with low college success rates.[11] In short: Poor college counseling plays a significant role here. "By closing existing gaps at the college level, especially the egregiously large gaps that exist in about one third of four-year institutions, we can cut that gap in half," writes report author Andrew Nichols.

So-called summer melt – the phenomenon by which students who were accepted to college and planned to attend don't show up for classes in the fall – contributes heavily to the gap, at an estimated 20 percent. And for low-income students, that rate doubles, says Melissa Fries, executive director of CAP, a California nonprofit that helps low-income students earn degrees.[12] One reason she cites for the significant summer melt among poor students is the startling high ratio of students to guidance counselors. In some high schools, a counselor can have caseloads of up to 900 students.

"Even if caseloads are reasonable, many counselors don't work during the summer, when a myriad of tasks need to be completed: submitting final transcripts, taking placement tests, signing up for housing, verifying financial aid information, and logging into their institution's online portal to register for orientation and complete other tasks," writes Fries. "Often, parents can't help either. Many juggle multiple jobs and are not native English speakers, and some don't know how to use a computer. For the most part, they haven't attended college themselves and can't navigate the complicated registration system."

COLLEGE COMPLETION A BLACK BOX FOR HIGH SCHOOLS

High school principals have never shown much interest in the college success rates of their alumni. They have enough on their plates just getting their students to earn high school diplomas. College success? Isn't that up to the alumni, their parents, and the colleges? Even if those high school leaders suddenly turned curious, they would have little data to draw from. Only two states, Georgia and Michigan, make available full data on whether graduates from specific high schools end up with college degrees, according to a 2018 report from the non-profit GreatSchools.

So Georgia and Michigan have turned the corner? Not exactly. In reality, anyone seeking that data will experience what I discovered when I tried to test the system by searching for college success information for a sampling of high schools located in both high- and low-income neighborhoods. On my own, I never found the right website. Finally, I tracked down the data expert in the Governor's Office of Student Achievement in Georgia, who led me to the relevant data dashboard. Even then, I struggled to complete what should have been a simple comparison of rich and poor schools.

If I had trouble, even with the state expert on the phone, what do parents from Georgia experience? As it turns out, that's not a problem, mostly because parents don't even realize the data is there, said Michael O'Sullivan, executive director of GeorgiaCAN, a school reform advocacy group. High schools don't make it available on their report cards. O'Sullivan said his group uses the data in presentations to parents, but generally, "it's not really out there."

There may be a reason why superintendents and principals don't like to share that data: It disrupts their narrative to parents that their districts and schools are wonderfully successful because their alumni go off to college. When Nicole Hurd's team from the College Advising Corps arrives at a school to pitch their college advising services, they come prepared with college success data culled from the National Student Clearinghouse. For a fee, the Clearinghouse will match high school graduation records against college records to determine who enrolled in college, who persisted, and who ended up earning degrees. Before sitting down with high school leaders, Hurd's team collects college graduation data.

"The most awkward conversation I've had, and the most heartbreaking, has been determining baseline data as we begin to partner with a school," said Hurd. "Ideally, we are able to collect [National Student Clearinghouse] data for three years to establish a baseline and then measure impact. A couple of times, I've had the awkward situation of sharing with a principal or team of educators the NSC data for the first time and it was lower than what they anticipated."

Hurd continues: "Unfortunately, schools often use self-reported data. For example, there may be an at end-of-the-year survey where they say 'How many of our students are going to college?' And the students raise their hands and then the school may record as many as 90 percent of their students are going to college. But then you run the NSC data and it may be as low as 50 percent who actually enrolled, and they look stunned. As much as this is an extremely tough moment, our message has been, 'We are not here to judge, we want to work with you and hold hands with you, and we're not going to know if we're being effective without baseline data.' But for a number of schools, establishing a baseline is a shocking moment."

Only rarely do we get a glimpse into any accurate college success rates for the big urban school districts, and that data doesn't usually come from the district itself. In late July 2018, we got a look at Newark Public Schools data, thanks to a report from the Newark City of Learning Collaborative and Rutgers University-Newark's School of Public Affairs and Administration that tracked 13,500 students who graduated from high school between 2011 and 2016.[13] The headline from the press coverage: "More Newark students are going to college, but only one in four earns degree within six years, new report finds."[14]

> **"**
>
> *Only rarely do we get a glimpse Into any accurate college success rates for the big urban school districts, and that data doesn't usually come from the district itself.*

There was good news in the press report: About half of Newark Public Schools students who graduated from high school between 2011 and 2016 went directly to college, compared with 39 percent of graduates from 2004 to 2010 who did that. And six years after leaving high school, 23 percent of the Class of 2011 had earned a college degree or certificate – more than double the rate of the Class of 2006. Sounds promising, but an online data supplement allowed an apples-to-apples national comparison with low-income students across the country who earned four-year degrees (not counting professional school certificates or two-year degrees). Among Newark's graduates who went to traditional comprehensive high schools, only 7.2 percent earned bachelor's degrees, compared with about 11 percent of low-income students nationally. Not surprisingly, those who went to a Newark magnet school fared better, with 33 percent earning four-year degrees. For the KIPP students in Newark, 31 percent earned degrees. Based on comparable studies in cities such as Chicago, there's reason to assume that similarly bad news would emerge from most urban districts, such as Los Angeles or Detroit or St. Louis.

COLLEGE: OVERRATED OR STILL THE BEST SHOT AT ESCAPING POVERTY?

Critics of the push to raise college success rates among low-income, minority, and first-generation students have an easy answer to these low success numbers: Why bother? College is overrated, likely to trigger punishing debts, and unlikely to produce jobs any better than skilled tradesmen. The country needs more plumbers, electricians, and welders, they argue.

The "college or bust" attitude of most education reformers is misplaced, argues Michael Petrilli, president of the Thomas B. Fordham Institute, a conservative education think tank.[15] "A better approach for many young people would be to develop coherent pathways beginning in high school, into authentic technical education options at the postsecondary level. But, right now, 81 percent of high school students are taking an academic route; only 19 percent are "concentrating" in career and technical education."

One quick glance at the dismal college success rates for low-income students should be enough to convince everyone that the college-for-all approach is not only misguided – it's not working, say the critics. Boosting trade schools and apprenticeships, not promoting bachelor's degrees, makes more sense for both the students and the country, they argue. The critics have a point; there are some quality vocational education programs, especially those done with business partners. Education Secretary Betsy DeVos embraces it as well, saying that the incessant push for four-year degrees overlooks trade schools. "To a large extent, we have stigmatized them for the past couple of decades. We have a lot of students who would benefit from being exposed to those different options." And Labor Secretary Alexander Acosta agrees.

Of course, the biggest "offenders" in the eyes of these critics are the charter school leaders, who even in the early grades pitch their schools to parents and teachers as their best bets for earning college degrees. We will pull your next generation out of poverty, they imply. Walk through any of the top charter elementary schools, and you'll see the college banners of the schools where the teachers earned their degrees. In some schools, the entire class gets nicknamed for the alma mater: Here's the "Amherst" class!

The charter leaders respond in two ways. The first answer, calm and pragmatic, is that yes, trades should be promoted. And some charters, including the Rooted School in New Orleans, are showing how that's done. But trade schools require literacy and math proficiency levels that in poor neighborhoods are best achieved by delivering a college preparation curriculum, they say.

The second response gets delivered in a more seething tone: Are those same advocates directing that message toward their own children and their friends' children? Why aren't we hearing that same advice aimed at high school students from wealthy suburban neighborhoods or those attending expensive private schools? Why does it come up only when we're talking about low-income, minority students? Don't the students and their families deserve some say here?

Charter leaders such as KIPP's Richard Barth are especially bothered by suggestions that charters should back away from their emphasis on earning college degrees. Barth wants KIPP to support students who choose non-college paths, but he says there are good reasons to emphasize college.[16]

He writes: "A college degree is the most reliable way we know of to break the cycle of intergenerational poverty. With a four-year college degree, over 40 percent of young people born into the U.S.'s lowest income quintile make the jump into the top two quintiles of income. With only a high school diploma, just 14 percent of young people in the lowest national income quintile will rise into the two top quintiles. Young people understand the payoff: Of the two-thirds of college-educated millennials who borrowed money to pay for their schooling, 86 percent say their degrees have been worth it or expect that they will pay off in the future."

My take on the trade-school-versus-college debate: The angry, visceral reaction you hear from charter leaders and other champions of the college path ("Are the critics steering their own children into the trades?") obscures the good points being made by those critics. Of course, students should have good options for pursuing a career that doesn't require a bachelor's degree. The tough reality, however, is that many high schools, especially those in high- poverty areas, aren't doing a good job preparing students for either a career or college.

In August 2018, those twin deficiencies got laid out in an Achieve report titled "Graduating Ready." A majority of college instructors report that fewer than half of recent high school graduates are adequately prepared in math and reading. And 61 percent of employers report that they require recent high school graduates to obtain additional education or training.

Attempts by states to fix those twin readiness problems, called college-and- career-ready (CCR) tracks, produce very different results. In Indiana, for example, where the CCR coursework is considered the

> **" A college degree is the most reliable way we know of to break the cycle of intergenerational poverty.**

default and students must opt out, 89 percent of all graduates pursue that track, including 86 percent of black students and 85 percent of Hispanic students. By contrast, in California, where students must opt in, just 47 percent of all graduates, 36 percent of black students, and 39 percent of Hispanic students complete the more rigorous CCR coursework.

As I learned from researching my book *Why Boys Fail*, it makes sense for many low-income students to embrace a college track curriculum, regardless of their ambitions.[17] That's the only way they can acquire sufficient literacy skills to handle trade school training programs. Here's a compromise to suggest for the quarreling camps: Starting with the charter networks (hopefully all high schools will join in eventually), begin citing three "success" outcomes for alumni: percent who earn professional certificates, percent who earn two-year degrees, and percent who earn bachelor's degrees.

Finally, we know from polling that first-generation college-goers see college as their ticket to a better life. For good reasons. Who's going to volunteer to tell them otherwise?[18]

COLLEGE IS THE NEW HIGH SCHOOL

IDEA co-founders JoAnn Gama and Tom Torkelson with students, 1999.
— *courtesy of IDEA Public Schools*

To put this simply, a breakthrough is not possible without first democratizing higher education.

By that I mean making college part of the expected-to-happen fabric of American life for all students, not just the students from well-off families. So what needs to take place to achieve it?

For starters, it means a change in mindset – recognizing that college is the new high school and that jobs that never before required a college degree now do, a phenomenon called college inflation or degree inflation. One study in 2015 from the Harvard Business School found that 67 percent of production supervisor job postings asked for college degrees – despite that only 16 percent of those who held the job at the time had a degree.[1]

Scores of jobs, ranging from bank tellers to the rental car workers who hand over your keys, have been subject to this inflation. Employers now assume that those renting a car expect to find a "professional" behind that counter, meaning someone with peer-like social skills. So they ask for college degrees, a rough guarantee that those abilities have been acquired. No wonder the need to earn a college degree has broadened.

There are some nascent signs that this trend may be turning around, that corporations are open to hiring non-degree earners for jobs that clearly don't require one – Starbucks supervisor and Apple store "Genius" are two examples – but change is very slow.[2] For the most part, and for years to come, there's no denying that college truly is the new high school for a vast number of American students who will end up in middle-income jobs.

It also means giving every student a high school education that's academically rigorous enough to avoid enduring classroom shock when exposed to college coursework. College "unreadiness" is a story that plays out in every state, with startling rates of unpreparedness in California, where more than half of high school graduates fail to meet the minimum requirements for the state universities.[3] But let's offer some quick examples from a state not normally associated with that problem, New York.[4] The odds of a student in the well-off suburbs going to a high school offering either International Baccalaureate or six or more Advanced Placement courses are

> "
> There's no denying that college truly is the new high school for a vast number of American students who will end up in middle-income jobs.

better than 90 percent. But in New York City, whose 1.1 million public school students are more likely to be poor and minority, those odds shrink to 18 percent.

It means everyone – students, parents, and colleges – should stop measuring a college's status based on how few students it lets in and shift to a model based on inclusivity. The aversion top colleges and universities exhibit toward taking transfer students, especially from community colleges, represents the worst kind of elitism.

It means financing education for low-income students to the extent that one car repair doesn't force them to drop out. KIPP's 2017 survey of its alumni revealed the extent of the problem: Nearly 60 percent of its alumni worry about running out of food, and more than 40 percent said they missed meals to pay for books, school fees, and other expenses.[5]

It means embracing the fact that college students of today are not the college students of yesterday. In 2015, the Georgetown Center on Education and the Workforce released "Learning While Earning," which laid out the new reality: About 14 million college students are working, with 70 percent of college students taking time away from college work to earn a paycheck.[6] In fact, U.S. students spend far more time working than in classrooms or studying. And yet few can work their way through college.[7] Even if a student worked full time at the federal minimum wage, that student would earn $15,080 annually. "Even if you work, you have to take out loans and take on debt," said Anthony Carnevale, director of the center.

What's needed, said report co-author Nicole Smith, is a tighter connection between work and learning. "When students pick a major or field of study, they need to be told up front what kind of career it likely leads to and how much money they are likely to make, especially if they have to pay back student loans." In 2018, the center updated the report to focus on how this disproportionately affects minority students.

It means counseling high school students to avoid college dropout factories, which are usually commuter universities with awful success rates. Nationally, the student-to-advisor ratio in high school is 482 to 1, and that doesn't account for the fact that most counselors have little time, and usually no training, to perform actual college advising. That lack of smart college guidance dooms thousands of students, thus perpetuating economic inequities. Like it or not, a degree appears to be the surest glide path to economic mobility. When a child born in the bottom fifth of the country's income distribution earns a college degree, their chances of making it to the top quintile nearly quadruple.

It means finding ways to make first-generation students feel welcome their freshman year rather than like strangers afloat in a sea of wealth. When interviewing the KIPP Gaston students from the Class of 2009, I was struck by the college shock nearly all felt after arriving on elite campuses, where most students spent freely and casually exchanged stories about expensive trips taken during school breaks – all while the first-generation students worried about getting bus fare for a trip home over Thanksgiving break. That's one reason so many of these students retreat to self-isolation on campus and socialize mostly with students like them. When it comes to classroom performance, where collaboration with other students, such as study groups, is essential, that isolation hurts them.

That's a formidable list, and it might even be considered fanciful except for one thing. There's a place in the United States where democratization of education has taken hold, and it's the most unlikely place you can imagine: the Rio Grande Valley in Texas, one of the poorest places in the country.

THEY SAID THEY WERE CRAZY: IDEA SHOOTS FOR 100% COLLEGE ACCEPTANCE

To outsiders, the area around McAllen, Texas is best known for other reasons: It's ground zero in the immigration wars. This is where Donald Trump wants to build the first part of his new border wall. It's home to the country's largest immigration detention center, the place where children infamously got separated from their parents. But there's another story playing out here. McAllen is also home to IDEA Public Charter Schools, a fast-growing charter network with ambitions that extend far beyond providing good K-12 schools. IDEA wants to democratize higher education, making it routine for thousands of low-income Hispanic families in the Rio Grande Valley, who never before even considered college. Based on my visits there, they are well on their way.

When IDEA founders Tom Torkelson and JoAnn Gama, both Teach for America teachers sent to the region (Tom, a student at Georgetown University, says he had trouble finding the place on a map), launched their first charter school in 2000 in Donna, the school was only grades 4-8, but the goal was always college: All our students will go to college. At that time, in a region where few of the low-income Hispanic students even thought college was a possibility, that promise couldn't pass a laugh test. "Everyone thought they were crazy," said Phillip Garza, who today oversees college programs for IDEA. "They said there was no way they could do it. But they had the courage and fortitude to get it done, and they delivered. For the last 12 years, 100 percent of our graduates have been accepted to college, and all but four students have gone."

Today, when driving through the region, it's not hard to spot billboards paid for by local school districts vowing that schools are all about "preparing students for college and careers." That's the impact IDEA has had in the Valley since 2000, said Garza. "Now, at all these districts, high school graduation alone is no longer the expectation." That's democratizing higher education. What this means on the ground is best viewed at the student level. Many middle-class suburban families might take one look at their stories and come to a quick judgment: These students are not college material. But that's not how IDEA sees them, and now it's not how the students see themselves.

Consider Ricardo Murillo, whose parents were deported to Mexico when he was 11. At the time, they were living in Edinburg, just outside McAllen. His mother sold ice cream; his father did everything from cutting grass to working as a handyman. His entire family moved back to Mexico, but when he was 13, Murillo – the only one born in the U.S. – concluded his future was brighter in the United States and returned to Texas, living with cousins outside Edinburg. After spending a summer in Mexico with his parents, he went back to Texas to learn that his cousins were transferring to an IDEA charter, and therefore he had to as well.

"I was pretty angry. IDEA was becoming a popular school, but it was not what I wanted. I thought it was a nerdy school." What Murillo wanted was to stay at his traditional public school in Donna, where, by his own description, he was becoming a "baggy" – a term for gang members and their baggy clothes. But he had no choice, so he entered IDEA Alamo. There, his grades ranged from C's to A's, depending on the course. It wasn't until his senior year that he even considered college, a must-do at IDEA.

Murillo ended up at the University of Texas Rio Grande Valley in Edinburg, best described as a commuter university. It's a choice embraced by many IDEA graduates, either because of middling grade point averages and test scores, a desire to live at home with family, or both. But UTRGV, as it is known locally, is a cut above the average commuter university. Torkelson sits on the board, and IDEA keeps two college counselors on campus just to guide its students.

The college success rate there – 40 percent of the entering freshmen earn a bachelor's degree within six years – is well below those of elite colleges and universities with success rates hitting the 90 percent mark. But that 40 percent is double what you find at many commuter universities, and IDEA's involvement probably has a lot to do with that.

Murillo still lives with a cousin, and he works at the homework center at an IDEA school, helping high school students with their studies. Despite his spotty record in middle school and high school, Murillo stepped it up in college, tackling a challenging electrical engineering major. He's on track to graduate in five years. With Pell Grants and scholarships, he will owe only about $4,000 after leaving college. After graduation, he's looking at two careers – taking a job at a robotics company or working as a school counselor at an IDEA school.

"An assistant principal at IDEA Alamo said I would make a great counselor, telling students about my background, how I made it," he said.

And then there's Juan Reyes, whose family has struggled with finances. He grew up in McAllen, then Pharr. His father worked as a furniture company driver, but the company went out of business. "He has diabetes, so it's hard to find work," Juan explains. His mother has always been a stay-at-home mom. Reyes went to district schools until ninth grade, when he switched to IDEA San Juan. "My parents didn't want me to go to [the local high school]. It was too violent, a lot of kids fighting."

At IDEA, the academic challenge was different. "At my neighborhood school, the teachers didn't care if you did the work. At IDEA, the teachers care. If you don't do the work, it's like you are hurting them." Reyes was a good student, not great. When it came time to choose a college – something that in earlier years had been hard to imagine – he also chose the University of Texas Rio Grande Valley. "My family was struggling, and Hispanic families are very close. When one member of the family leaves, everyone is sad. So it would have been hard for me to leave."

Much like Murillo, when Reyes got to UTRGV he stepped it up, enrolling in the accounting program. He has nearly a 3.0 grade point average, and in the summer of 2018, he was only one course away from graduation. He will leave with about $8,000 in college debt. His goal: a master's degree in accounting and a job as an accountant at a university.

Both Murillo and Reyes represent what's happening in the Rio Grande Valley, courtesy of IDEA charters. Yes, IDEA sends a fair number of its graduates to the more prestigious University of Texas at Austin and

Texas A&M and a sprinkling to the Ivies and other top Eastern universities [my personal favorite: several years ago, when watching a raucous college signing day at a local arena, I saw Gilberto Gutierrez celebrate his acceptance at MIT. His mother works at an IDEA school cafeteria]. But that's not really what democratization of higher education is all about. What democratization does mean is that over the past 12 years, as Garza points out, 100 percent of IDEA's students have been accepted to colleges, and all but four have gone, thanks in part to universities such as UTRGV.

The question to ask, of course, is: Are they successful? Do they earn degrees? Over those 12 years, roughly 44 percent of IDEA graduates ended up with bachelor's degrees. For comparison purposes, roughly 11 percent of low-income students do the same. Even more interesting: Like other charter networks, IDEA tracks its graduates by cohorts. For the more recent Class of 2012, the projection shows that 55 percent are on track to earn a bachelor's within six years, the highest in the network's history.

Should IDEA worry that so many of its graduates end up at UTRGV? That question gets at the heart of what democratization of education means. Garza loves to cite the number of graduates who go off to prestigious colleges, where the likelihood of earning degrees is near certainty. But he also knows his IDEA families, who struggle with financial issues and grapple even more with seeing any of their children leave town. "College is an academic decision, but it's also a fiscal decision and a social decision," said Garza. "We are in the business of 'me power' ... We want to give families choices." And if they choose to stay close to home and graduate nearly debt-free, so be it. It was an informed choice.

IDEA's push for the democratization of higher education extends to gathering up students who "stopped out" of college and want another shot. In what is called IDEA-U, students sign up for the online curriculum offered by College for America at Southern New Hampshire University. But instead of a problematic do-it-alone-at-home online program, IDEA-U offers an actual classroom building complete with a tutor/counselor. Not only can the students escape home distractions, but they have the kind of education technology, including computers, that aren't found in their homes. The tuition is $5,500 a year, which matches a Pell Grant, and IDEA predicts that most of its students will complete an associate's degree in eight to 14 months.

What makes the College for America program work for low-income students, said Paul LeBlanc, president of Southern New Hampshire University, is that it's competency-based. Mastering the content is what counts, he said, not mastering the content in a prescribed period of time, which is the way most colleges operate. "When a student's daughter has a bout of illness, they can just stop out. There's no penalty for hitting the pause button. When they are ready to begin again, they hit the start button."

The coaches based at IDEA-U are about more than academics, said LeBlanc. "They are life coaches. If you are poor, society is sending you signals all day long that you don't matter very much. Because if you did matter, you would have a decent grocery store in your neighborhood. If you did matter, people would care more about the plight of the poor in America."

The coaches and the academic center offer a sense of belonging, a sense that you do matter – a sentiment these students rarely feel, said LeBlanc. "It's no surprise kids join gangs. The gangs tell them that you matter so much they would kill for you. It's a signal that you matter, that you belong." The coaches, said LeBlanc, are always talking to the students. "They're asking about their learning, how things are at home, how they did on that last project. And the students think, 'Oh, wow, somebody cares that I'm doing this."

IDEA-U opened in 2017 with 100 students. The goal: 6,000 students in six years with multiple centers. A fanciful goal, perhaps, for anyone other than IDEA, but this is the fastest-growing charter network in the country, and it has always met its expansion plan. Currently, IDEA has 79 schools with 48,000 students and aims to have 100,000 students in 200 schools by the year 2022.

> "
>
> *The coaches and the academic center offer a sense of belonging, a sense that you do matter — a sentiment these students rarely feel.*

IDEA offers an insight into Phase Two of *The B.A. Breakthrough.* Phase One was the push to do right by students who are talented but poor, those who graduate at the top of their high school classes, test well, but rarely make it to a college that's their equal, a college from which they are likely to graduate. The Jack Kent Cooke Foundation, which seeks out these students for scholarships, estimates there are 3.4 million high-ability, low-income students in grades K-12.[8] That's a lot, and the foundation deserves thanks for its pioneering work. But all those talented kids have siblings and neighborhood friends who attend school with them. Reaching all those students and finding a college pathway for all of them, not just the very brightest, is what IDEA and other charters do. That's Phase Two of the Breakthrough.

Nobody believed Tom Torkelson and JoAnn Gama when they opened their first charter and promised college for all. Not only have they done that with their own alumni, but they forced the traditional school districts in the region to pursue the same college-for-all goal. The Rio Grande Valley is not the only place in the United States where the democratization movement is playing out. California is a close runner-up.

But the Rio Grande Valley may be the only place where you can read all about it on billboards.

2

BUILDING THE BREAKTHROUGH

REVERSE ENGINEERING K-12 FOR COLLEGE SUCCESS

Michael Mann, head of school, North Star Academy College
Preparatory High School, Newark, N.J., teaching Target 3.0
— *photo by Richard Whitmire*

CHAPTER 4

In the charter school universe, Newark's North Star Academy is fabled.

It was one of the first high-performing charter schools, launched in 1997 with 72 students, succeeding with students growing up in a city that most Americans believe died long ago. And it is one of the most visited charter schools in the country. Charter startup entrepreneurs across the U.S. adopted parts of the morning Community Circle pioneered here, a mashup involving African drums, call and response, academic exercises, and awards – all fast-paced and loud, very loud. It sets the day for students and staff. It works.

North Star, part of Uncommon Schools, has been home to school leader Michael Mann for about 20 years. Over that time, he has invented and reinvented curriculum, discipline, school culture, pretty much everything that needed doing to succeed with students coming from challenging urban environments. And yet, after all those years, he was still watching a small percentage of high school students struggle and fail. Why?

> "
>
> *And yet, after all those years, he was still watching a small percentage of high school students struggle and fail. Why?*

As with any top charter network, success and failure are ultimately defined by college completion: How many of our students end up earning college degrees? College graduation is what parents are promised; it's what makes these charters, with their longer hours and tougher discipline, palatable. One thing North Star discovered in its quest to understand why some students floundered trying to reach that goal was something that seems, on the surface, almost too simplistic to matter: North Star graduates with grade point averages above 3.0 are four times as likely to earn college degrees.

It was a pretty stark statistic: *four times* as likely. It couldn't be ignored. As it turns out, all the student strategies involved in learning how to raise your GPA are the exact tactics students will need to persist in college. "Your GPA is the ultimate measure of grit in high school. That's all about work ethic, about your ability to persevere," said Paul Bambrick-Santoyo, who oversees Uncommon's high school and professional development programs.

It's not that test scores matter less. In fact, Uncommon found that raising SAT scores pushed up college success rates. "While we may fight it, the SAT is a very objective measure of college readiness. English and math are the foundations," said Bambrick-Santoyo. In 2005, the average combined math and verbal score for North Star seniors was 932 out of a perfect 1600. Since 2012, the average scores have never dropped below 1,000, the result of programs designed to improve the SAT outcomes of North Star students.

"Those 70 points are more than marginal," Bambrick-Santoyo said. "Our students have been dramatically more successful at handling college work when they've gotten above that bar." Especially important, he said, was the SAT verbal score. "If you can't read at [a] level to get a 500 [out of 800] on the SAT, you can't handle college-level reading work, especially scientific articles."

One of the major issues North Star teachers identified was that instead of thinking critically for themselves, many students would just listen and use the analyses of the one or two students who spoke up during class. As a result, all the students were able to write decent papers – but without ever truly understanding the meaning of what they were writing. They were getting free rides off those couple of students, a ride not available to them on tests or independent reading exercises.

That discovery led to an instructional change: After students finished a new reading, they wrote their own analyses first and discussed it in class later.

But test scores still don't trump GPA. That's the conclusion of a recent study by Matthew M. Chingos, director of the Urban Institute's Education Policy Program. The study, part of a "What Matters Most for College Completion" project, also settled on grades as the most important predictor.[1]

"Both SAT or ACT scores and high school GPA are associated with the likelihood that students at four-year colleges earn a bachelor's degree. But when considered together, the predictive power of high school GPA is much stronger," writes Chingos:

> *This makes sense given that earning good grades requires consistent behaviors over time – showing up to class and participating, turning in assignments, taking quizzes, etc. – whereas students could in theory do well on a test even if they do not have the motivation and perseverance needed to achieve good grades. It seems likely that the kinds of habits high school grades capture are more relevant for success in college than a score from a single test.*

The path that North Star took to boost student GPAs is only one of many strategies adopted by top charters to drive college success rates. Not to mention exposing students and parents to college counseling. There are too many to detail all in depth, so I will focus on just this one, raising the GPA, because it reveals much about the hard work, surprises, adjustments, and readjustments that go into the process of increasing college success. Truly, this is rocket science.

SOLVING A MYSTERY: THE LINK BETWEEN ABSENCES AND FAILURE

Why, after all these years, was Mike Mann, North Star's head of school, still seeing students with poor grade point averages? He knew two of the reasons: poor work ethic and learning disabilities. When he first began working on the issue, he didn't suspect there was a third, undiscovered reason. Poor work ethic is an obvious one any educator knows about. Its most recognizable symptom: not completing homework.

"Some parents struggle in getting their children to do their homework, and the students are unmotivated. So that's one reason," said Mann. "The second, learning disabilities, is another obvious one. These are the students who are highly motivated, turn in all their homework, and still fail on tests. We know that one well. We have things in place, both in general education and special education, to address that."

But Mann suspected there was a third reason. "For a long time, I couldn't find it. It was like dark matter; it took me a long time." Eventually, the dark matter revealed itself to be absences. When students who were already doing poorly were absent, they lacked the motivation to check in with their teachers to see what work they missed. They just let it slide, which means that day's assignment registered as a blank in the teacher's grade point records. On the surface, the student's grades might seem OK, but at the end of the marking period, when the teacher pushed the button on the laptop to calculate the grade, all those blanks became zeros. The result was an awful or failing grade that was too late to do anything about.

"We hadn't seen this before," said Mann. "As a result, we weren't taking care of it." So Mann set out to correct the problem. In the student dashboard, where students can view all their coursework and current grades, there's now a second column, right after the homework completion column, that cites unfinished work. Now, there's no hiding from it. Plus, the school designed a new grading system for teachers, so that they enter zeros right away, rather than leaving blanks. Again, no hiding from it.

STUDENTS CONFRONT THEIR SHORTCOMINGS AND BOOST THEIR GPAS

The Target 3.0 program at North Star is Mann's baby. He designed it; he teaches it; he invented the remedy and then he reinvented the remedy when it was clear he was on the wrong track. On the day I visited, the class of 72 students (out of 614 in the school) included every student in the 10th, 11th, and 12th grades with a GPA less than 2.5. Think about that for a moment: The lowest-performing students, all (unhappily) gathered in a very large room with a single teacher. In most schools that's a recipe for a disaster – unruly students and a teacher who bails out at the end of the year, if not before. That's why Mann took it on himself.

Mann cites three reasons for being personally involved in turning around the GPAs of his lowest-performing students. First, he's the creator, so he's constantly tinkering with it. Target 3.0 required inventing a new student data dashboard. Uncommon didn't have one, but Noble Network of Charter Schools in Chicago did, so Mann knew he would have to borrow and adapt – something a school leader has the clout to do. Second, the students wouldn't take it seriously unless the school leader did it. Third, he learned a lot – such as discovering the mysterious reason why some student GPAs took a sudden plunge when teachers pressed the calculate-GPA button.

The students file in and sit at assigned tables, or "teams," where they must talk about their lagging grade point averages. It's called an "accountability conversation," and each student describes a "smart goal" for turning things around in their worst class. The following week, they will have to explain how they met, or didn't meet, that goal. To make sure the questioning is unsparing, Mann provides a script for the students to read as they address fellow students: "The script language is pretty blunt. We think that makes it sound more real. And at the beginning of the semester, we make them practice the script. They go through the whole script: 'OK, you said you would go in to see Miss Dash to get the quiz done. Is it done? No? So you were either lying to us or something else happened.'" Why? If parental pressure doesn't work, and teacher pressure doesn't work, maybe peer pressure will have an impact.

There's no escaping having your personal "stuff" aired in a Target 3.0 class. Peer pressure is pretty much the whole point, starting with the name of every student [if he or she grants permission] projected on a giant screen, accompanied by their GPA. That's on top of lots of color-coded papers students receive (not to be shared with others) that lay out every detail about their academic life at North Star. Many use their own cell phones to track their successes and failures using PowerSchool, a how-you're-doing-in-school online platform that can be shared with parents. Like I said, there's no hiding here. After all the data accountability demands get met, some students are dispatched to visit teachers to settle how those assignment "blanks" get filled in, thus avoiding the zero debacle.

It all seems to work, especially with the older, more mature students. Within a semester, all the seniors boost their GPAs above a 2.5. For juniors, that rate is 74 percent. Only half the sophomores make the leap. That will change, Mann assures me, as students advance through the grades.

Senior Malaya Pleasant is blunt about her past failings. "For my first two or three years of high school, I just never cared. I know that's bad, but for years I didn't. In the beginning years of high school, I didn't realize that, oh, I have to go to college after this, that I have to prepare my GPA in order to do something after high school. So I struggled a lot. I took Advanced Placement classes that I wasn't ready to handle."

For the past two years, she has been in Mann's Target 3.0 classes. Her turning point came this year when Mann chose her as a group leader, one of the students in charge of each small group that sits together in the large classroom. Helping other struggling students prompted her to improve. "So I got my agenda [a record of all school assignments, test days, etc.] and started writing down my homework every day. Organization is key. Like, if you're not organized, I don't know how you survive."

She found herself in charge of helping three students: a transfer from another school, a student with behavior problems who was chronically absent, and a student who seemed to have no purpose in school. "That last one was similar to me, so I connected with him the most."

She made progress with that student, and she is meeting with the student with behavior problems. "I'm asking why he's acting out and why he is not utilizing the resources the North Star gave him to succeed."

But the biggest turnaround may be herself. Being asked to be a leader was something special, something that had never happened to her. At the beginning of her senior year, her GPA was a 2.4. By the time I visited, in April of 2018, it was up to a 2.7. "By the end of the year, I'm trying to get at least a 2.8 or 2.9. My target is 3.0, but I know that's kind of unrealistic."

"

By the end of the year, I'm trying to get at least a 2.8 or 2.9. My target is 3.0, but I know that's kind of unrealistic.

Already, college is firmly in her future. She has acceptances from Stockton University in Galloway, New Jersey, and Morgan State University in Baltimore, Maryland. Her goal: to become a forensic psychologist.

Sophomore Alex Lopez has been at North Star for five years. "My first two years were not the best. I have always struggled with science and math because I was never good with numbers." Little things, such as making sure he wrote down everything in his personal agenda, helped him complete homework. And making sure he did his homework at school, in a study hall period, rather than at home, helped as well. At home, other distractions, such as the TV or the phone, were too strong a pull. Often he would forget about homework assignments until late at night. "Then I would stay up until 2 a.m. trying to do homework and come to school tired with only four hours of sleep." Since that shift, he's been getting to bed around 10 p.m.

Currently, Lopez's GPA is a 2.33. Even though college is two years away, he's aware that his current grade point average falls short of dream acceptances, such as Boston College, which he thinks would require a 3.6 or higher. "I don't want to stress over that because I know if I start stressing then I'm going to overwork myself, and when I do that, everything just becomes a mess."

TEACHING K-12 KIDS COLLEGE SURVIVAL SKILLS

The college success strategies at most of the big charter networks resemble one another, which is not surprising considering the cross-fertilization among them. At KIPP, a leader in pushing hard for better college completion, three strategies emerged. First, the network departed from its middle-school-only playbook and expanded in both directions, elementary and high school. The reason is simple: A student who stayed with KIPP through high school had a far better chance of earning a degree than a student who only went to a KIPP middle school. KIPP also built an elaborate KIPP Through College program that uses college selection science to pick just the right school for its graduates and then tracks them through college, using specially adapted software from Salesforce, which writes software for businesses.

And KIPP also embraced the findings of researchers such as Angela Duckworth, who pioneered a self-reliance strategy popularly known as grit. Her research lined up with what KIPP co-founder Dave Levin had noticed early on, that the students most likely to earn degrees weren't necessarily those with the best academic records. Rather, they were the students with resilience, an ability to bounce back after a bad grade, the students outgoing and confident enough to seek out help from professors.

These were the students most likely to make the transition from the hyper-controlled high school experiences at KIPP to the anything-goes realities of a college campus. KIPP's "character counts" program led to the posting outside all classrooms of the seven "strengths" that need developing beyond competency in math and reading. They are: zest, grit, optimism, self-control, gratitude, social intelligence, and curiosity.

At other charter networks, the changes made to boost college success might look a little different, but they share one commonality: making students more independent learners and thus more likely to survive on a college campus. At Boston's Brooke Charter Schools, for example, which just launched its first high school and has yet to send any graduates to college, the mindset begins in the earliest grades.

During one visit there, I watched fourth-grade teacher Heidi Deck practice "flipped instruction," in which students, when presented with a new problem, are first asked to solve it on their own, armed only with the tools of lessons learned from previous problems. "We really push kids to be engaged with the struggle," said Deck. Next, she invites them to collaborate with one another to solve the problem, followed by more individual attempts to do the same. Always, Deck expects the students to figure out the puzzle.

This is exactly the opposite of the most common approach to instruction, in which teachers demonstrate and then have students practice what they just watched. That's dubbed the "I do – we do –

you do" approach. With flipped instruction – and the many other teacher innovations here – "kids have to do the logical work of figuring something out rather than repeating what the teacher does," said Brooke's chief academic officer, Kimberly Steadman. The goal: Starting with its Class of 2020, the first graduating class Brooke sends off to college, all its students will be independent learners, able to roll with the surprises that confront all college students, especially first-generation college-goers.

Preparing students to be self-directed learners, regardless of whether they pursue college or a career, is at the heart of the radically different Summit Learning program, which grew out of the Summit charter schools in Silicon Valley. As happened at many charter networks, Summit discovered its college success rate was lower than expected, in part because its students were too micromanaged in high school. In short, a failure to create self-directed learners.

To create academic independence that will help their alumni make their way through college to win a degree, Summit shifted to self-directed learning, coordinated by sophisticated software developed with the help of Facebook engineers. There's some traditional teaching, but often the teachers act more as facilitators, tutors, or advisers. Rather than expand its charters, Summit chose to grow by offering its learning program to both charter and traditional district schools. As of the summer of 2018, the Summit program was being used at 330 schools in 40 states and the District of Columbia.

At Rhode Island's Blackstone Valley Prep, I watched 15-year-old Ray Varone use the program on his Chromebook. He could view all his courses, including projects done, projects completed, and tests yet to be taken. A vertical "pacer line" shows him exactly where he stands in each course. For resources, he can draw from hundreds of "playlists," which are learning tools such as online instructional videos from Khan Academy to help with math problems.

"We're getting used to doing this on our own," Varone told me. "In college, you're not going to have teachers there asking you questions all the time, so you have to learn by yourself."

That's what self-directed learning is all about, and it's what the charter networks hope will push up their college success rates with first-generation students. To date, the data suggest it's helping.

THE MOST IMPORTANT COLLEGE SUCCESS INNOVATOR YOU'VE NEVER HEARD OF

Matt Niksch with robotic students from Rauner College Prep,
part of Chicago's Noble Network of Charter Schools
— *courtesy of Noble Network of Charter Schools*

CHAPTER 5

In my 2016 book, *The Founders*,[1] I tried to track down all the people

who had something to do with creating the big charter management organizations that were making a difference in the lives of poor, minority students. Among education reform insiders, the names were mostly familiar: Don Shalvey, the Californian who sparked the sprawling network of charters in that state; KIPP co-founders Dave Levin and Mike Feinberg and CEO Richard Barth; the co-founders of North Star Academy Charter Schools in Newark, Norman Atkins and Jamey Verrilli; Dacia Toll from Achievement First; and the co-founders of IDEA, Tom Torkelson and JoAnn Gama. By the end of the book, the list of major players grew to well over a hundred. Nowhere in *The Founders*, however, was the name Matt Niksch.

Based on the interviewing for this book, I can now admit that was an omission. In the world of charter school breakthroughs in college success, which I believe is their biggest contribution in the education field, Niksch (pronounced as in New York Knicks) is one of the biggest names out there – and the biggest name you've probably never run across.

Niksch occupies a unique position. He's not a charter school founder, nor an operator. He's a software guy, and his college-advising software programs, written for his Chicago-based Noble Network, have spread throughout the charter networks and now appear likely to get adopted by traditional school districts. A graduate of Purdue University, Niksch trained as an aerospace and electrical engineer. His father, also a Purdue graduate, was an aeronautical engineer; his mother graduated from Purdue with a degree in mathematics.

During college, he designed microchips for Advanced Micro Devices, a semiconductor company, and then after college worked for Lockheed Martin while picking up a master's degree in electrical engineering from Virginia Tech. Still searching for the ideal career, he earned his MBA from the University of Chicago and worked as a business consultant at McKinsey & Company.

Not finding anything he was passionate about in his private sector search, Niksch concluded that education was the right path. His mother was a math teacher in the district he had attended, and later Niksch had worked as a substitute teacher during college breaks. "I'd also recently seen some of the research on student growth showing that 'low-performing' students were generally the same as 'high-performing' students – the difference was the quality of the schooling they received," said Niksch. "I'd also recently had my first child, and I worried about the moral example I'd be setting for him if I knew there was no fundamental difference between him and the young people growing up a few block east of us in Chicago, and yet tacitly accepting the idea that the outcomes would be different."

His jump into education happened in 2009 when he landed a Broad Residency in Urban Education, which offers training to potential "game-changer" leaders, many of them recruited from outside education. That residency connected Niksch to KIPP and its KIPP to College research, which at that point in time was far ahead of what any school network was doing, charter or traditional. Soon after, the program was renamed KIPP Through College, a change that emphasized the refocus from college *acceptance* to college *completion*. At KIPP, Niksch teamed up with Craig Robinson, now with the College Advising Corps, at a unique time in KIPP's history.

In the beginning years, KIPP's leaders just assumed that a focus on academic rigor and winning college acceptances for its students would lead to more college degrees. Their philosophy had been to execute the basic "block and tackle" process that everyone believed would work: Fill out the application, complete the federal financial aid form, track down teachers for recommendations, make sure all the standardized testing gets done, ask for fee waivers when possible. But their philosophy that students were automatically ready for college and could enroll and earn a degree without any additional support only led to modest success. "After we went through all those steps, we sort of faced this reality," said Robinson, "that students who were able to get to college weren't making it through. And sometimes we'd see that early, in the first year at the end of the first semester."

As KIPP discovered in 2011, only about a third of its students, while excelling academically in high school, ended up with college degrees. The fact that this was nearly three times the rate for low-income students provided only weak consolation. It was a clear setback, and KIPP debated what to do with the news. The choice: Say nothing publicly while shifting resources to correct the problem or go public so everyone knew about a shortfall that was not unique to KIPP. They chose to go public. "We felt it was important to be honest about our learnings," said Robinson.

But KIPP had more than full disclosure in mind; it wanted to generate solutions, both for its own students and others. Thus, KIPP Through College shifted into high gear – an effort that spanned all grades and went beyond just academic readiness. The broader goal: infuse students with the grit to tough out college challenges and the joy to make schoolwork less of a grind. But the key components of KTC involved choosing the right college and tracking the students once they left high school.

"We knew that some colleges are just way better than others in helping kids complete, so we started investing resources to systematically solve the challenge we had seen with our alumni not finishing college," said Niksch. "Working with Craig Robinson, we came up with the idea of trying to do data-driven college counseling." Generally, high schools recruit college counselors for their empathy skills, the heart and soul of the profession. The plan: Equip those counselors with software tools so they could bring heart, soul – and head – to the profession.

In reviewing the data on where their students were most likely to succeed, they discovered that colleges within the same "band"– meaning near-identical colleges with similar acceptance rates – often had radically different graduation rates, as much as a 20-percentage-point difference. For KIPP college counselors, that was revelatory. When counselors first make contact with students about their college plans, beginning in junior year and intensifying in senior year, there's little they can do to boost the student's academic profile. Grade point averages are tough to raise in a short period of time, extracurriculars are difficult to add on at the last minute, and standardized test scores might improve somewhat on re-taking, but nothing radical enough to propel a student from, say, a competitive college to a more selective college, where the graduation odds are higher. However, steering a student into a college in the same selectivity band that has a higher graduation rate – that's huge.

At this point, the KTC process became a software challenge – something Niksch had spent a lifetime preparing for. Niksch developed some early college matching software for KIPP, but KIPP at the time was a collection of small charter management organizations grouped nationally by geographic region with a limited sample size of alumni old enough to be earning degrees. Thus, the research challenge was formidable. "You can't just write a program that says every kid has to go to a school with a 50 percent graduation rate [at the six-year mark]," Niksch said. "That might work in Illinois, where the graduation rate at the University of Illinois in Chicago is just north of 50 percent, but in Tennessee, outside of Vanderbilt, all these school are below that. National dictates are really tricky."

Niksch, who was living in Chicago at the time, met a principal from Noble who asked him for advice on college guidance for his founding senior class. Unlike KIPP, which at the time was just launching high schools, Noble had started out with high schools. Immediately, Niksch recognized that Noble possessed the research base he was looking for – thousands of alumni already in college and beyond, all in a single city, Chicago. So in 2012 when Noble opened up a college success advising position, Niksch jumped at it. "I told the KIPP folks, 'Hey, we've been trying to solve this problem for a while, and it's hard to do here. I'm going to use what they have at Noble to move forward in figuring this out and will share back what we learn." As documented in *The Founders*, sharing among the big networks was common, and KIPP and Noble were especially close.

With Noble's database, Niksch made quick progress. Within a few months, he had all the information he needed to form this kind of calculation: For instance, if a student has a 3.3 GPA and a 21 on the ACT, his odds of getting into the University of Illinois might be 31 percent. By late August 2012, Niksch rolled out a predictive tool he named College Counseling Bot 2000 – the "Bot" came from thinking of a kid-friendly robot making college admission predictions. Immediately, Noble counselors had a powerful tool that showed the odds a student had of getting admitted into a certain college based on their academic record. Matching those odds against the college success records of a particular college, counselors could guide students into not just the top-ranked college they were likely to get into but also the top-ranked college where they were most likely to win degrees. As promised, Niksch shared the program with KIPP, and the world of data-driven college counseling suddenly became a reality.

At Noble, the difference was immediate. Before the Bot , a student might apply to eight colleges – let's say six sure bets and two extreme reaches (translation: basically, no chance of getting in). The result: that student landed at a "sure bet" college. In the parlance of college counseling, that's called "underreaching." The problem with underreaching is that lesser-ranked "sure bet" colleges are also less likely to monitor student success, which means students are less likely to earn degrees. A "reach" college, one that's more challenging to get into, generally has higher graduation rates. With the Bot, that same student was targeting better colleges, avoiding the extreme reaches and the under-matching sure bets. The result: More of their alumni earned degrees.

> **"**
>
> *With the Bot, that same student was targeting better colleges, avoiding the extreme reaches and the under-matching sure bets.*

One unexpected side benefit from the Bot, greatly appreciated by the counselors, was that it informed students when they were overreaching, thus allowing the counselor to avoid that unpleasantness. "You find kids with a 2.5 GPA and 18 on the ACT say to the counselor: 'I'm going to Harvard because Michelle Obama said I could.'" With the Bot software, it was a goofy robot informing the student that that wasn't going to happen. For some reason, the tough love proved to be easier to hear from a robot than from a counselor.

A SOFTWARE PROGRAM THAT FINDS THE 'MONEY SCHOOLS'

The next software program developed by Niksch was a program that tracked the "historical affordability" of colleges. By collecting the financial award letters sent to Noble seniors, Niksch was able to calculate which colleges, from the nearly 200 that Noble seniors applied to, offered workable financial packages. By 2013, he had a tool counselors could use to guide students in that direction – toward the colleges dubbed "money schools." By combining the affordability program with the predictive admissions program, the counselors got a powerful selection tool to share with students and parents.

Niksch offered a hypothetical example from Illinois. A student attending the University of Illinois is looking at $32,000 for tuition, room, and board. A low- income student from Illinois would pull in about $10,000 in state and federal grants, and the university would provide another $18,000 in institutional grants (essentially a discount). If the student took about $4,000 in federal loans, that would cover the entire cost. Now compare that to the private Knox College in Galesburg, where the same math exercise would conclude that the student would owe an additional $6,000. Worth it to go to a private school? Not really, because the University of Illinois actually has a higher graduation rate than Knox. "That's a pretty easy choice, because the University of Illinois is a great school, and it's really affordable." But compared to another in-state university, with a lower graduation rate but similar affordability – let's say Millikin University in Decatur or Augustana College in Rock Island – then Knox starts looking like the wiser choice.

Suddenly, counselors at Noble, KIPP, and elsewhere have more than heart and soul. They have data that pops up immediately on the computer screen. Now they have head, heart, and soul.

The software program, now called the Decision Report, also got shared with KIPP and others. The original Bot software, adapted to their particular needs, is used by nearly all the top charter networks. Also in Niksch's toolkit: the Weekly Report (within Noble, called the SSV, for Single Student View). Students come up with their initial list of favored colleges, but that list changes quickly, which led Niksch to write software that tracks the changing list, giving updates on a student's odds of getting into newly listed colleges, and the affordability of those places. This new addition to the arsenal is far more powerful than the original Bot. "It almost ensures that kids are going to have great choices come spring," Niksch said. This, also, is getting shared with other networks.

'IT'S REALLY ABOUT ALL THE STUDENTS, NOT JUST THE STUDENTS YOU SERVE'

There's more to Niksch's Skunk Works-like list of disruptive innovations: the Alumni Tool, which has roots in his time spent at KIPP. When thinking about how to support alumni in college, Niksch discovered that high school counselors charged with tracking those students were drowning in data and asking for Excel spreadsheet training. "I thought that was ridiculous. I don't want people whose job it is to be good at helping and supporting kids to be super-focused on being good at Excel." So back in 2009 the KIPP team hired consultants to modify business software from Salesforce, experts in what's know as customer relationship management, to produce an alumni tracking system.

Now at Noble, Niksch was able to recreate a "quick and dirty" copy of what he had developed at KIPP, improve and update it, and apply it to Noble alumni. The task was made less difficult because its

> " I don't want people whose job it is to be good at helping and supporting kids to be super-focused on being good at Excel.

students all came from the Chicago area and most went to a relatively small group of colleges and universities. Today, about 20 CMOs all over the country use the Noble alumni database tool, which grew out of the KIPP program, to track about 100,000 of their students. Once a new network wants to adopt the software, Niksch said, it takes only a two-hour conference call for him to help them set it up.

Niksch, a boyish, self-effacing Midwesterner, who looks far younger than 42, has this reaction to the impact he's having: "I mean, it's kind of neat." As for measuring the results of his program, he conservatively puts the bump in college graduation rates at somewhere between 5 and 10 percent. At Noble, which has an alumni population of more than 10,000 students, that's between 500 and 1,000 students getting bachelor's degrees who might otherwise not have just because, as Niksch puts it, "We made a goofy bot."

It's important to keep in mind that his software programs are getting deployed across the country by charter networks, and they appear likely to break through in traditional school districts, which are just acknowledging that they own, at least partly, the college fate of their alumni. It doesn't pay as well as designing chips or aerospace systems, but Niksch seems OK with that.

The key to having real impact with the software programs was keeping them non-proprietary. Although it seems like a given now that these programs are meant to be shared, it didn't have to be that way. What Niksch invented has real value and, if kept proprietary, could have been, to use the Silicon Valley lingo, monetized. That was never even considered, said Robinson, Niksch's former colleague at KIPP. "The folks who are committed to this work learn pretty quickly that if you want to be transformative at scale, you've got to open your doors. You have to open source. And if you're sharing, you are also receiving learning. It's part of a community practice. It's really about all the students, not just the students you serve."

INSIDE THE SCHOOL WITH THE COUNTRY'S PRICIEST ALUMNI TRACKING SYSTEM

Clearly, KIPP has the most evolved – and expensive – tracking system in the country. And within the KIPP network, its NYC College Prep high school in the Bronx probably fields the most sophisticated counseling/ tracking operation.

In 2017, to report The Alumni series, I visited the school to get a snapshot of a typical day there.[2] In all my charter school visits, I'd never seen anything like it. At this high school on the day I was there, a dozen counselors were working as a team on the task of college completion – some handling college advising, others tracking alumni through college. This doesn't come cheap: Just on the tracking operation alone, KIPP was spending $2,000 per student per year. In the coming years, as its alumni population grows, the plan is to trim that back to $1,600 per student. KIPP, unlike other networks, tracks all its middle school graduates, regardless of whether they went to a KIPP high school or not, which greatly increases the number of students it follows and undoubtedly reduces its overall college success rate. Their leaders do it because they believe it's the right thing to do.

During my visit, I sat down with Tessa Kratz, director of college and career counseling, who laid out a student-by-student college matching strategy that was as intricate as anything I came across during my years reporting on the Pentagon. Her campaign starts in the student's junior year when parents coming to report card night are asked to bring their tax forms, which get scanned into the system – the first of many building blocks needed to find the right-match college with the right-match financial aid package.

I also sat in on a college prep class for juniors, where two visiting KIPP alumni described their college experiences. There was no sugarcoating here. One of the alums described a searing experience of isolation and academic failure that led to her transferring to another college and downsizing her career expectations. This is what can happen when things go wrong, said the alum. The other alum advised the students against tuning out the incessant college advice they got. That's advice you may desperately need when you land on a college campus, she told the juniors. "KIPP is just letting you know what the real world is like."

I also sat in on a college prep class for seniors run by the KIPP Through College team, the counselors the students will stay in touch with once they arrive on campus. More tough-love talk here about staying out of trouble by avoiding peer pressure, with the counselors warning that, unlike students from wealthy families, they don't have the same leeway to mess up and recover. "We've got your back, but we're not heroes. If you get kicked out, it's going to be hard to get you back in," the counselor told them, listing all the scholarships and grants that keep them afloat. "We don't have the luxury of just moving you to another college."

The entire package, while expensive, seems to be working: 46 percent of the graduates from this high school are earning bachelor's degrees, about four times the rate of students from similar backgrounds.

Although the college advising tactics seen at KIPP are common at all the top charter networks, the college tracking teams vary widely. Few choose (or are able) to invest the money that KIPP does. The most interesting contrast is found with Uncommon Schools, where Newark's North Star Academy has long been regarded as an exemplary charter. But several years ago, the North Star team looked at the rising numbers of alumni and the cost of following them through college, and decided to invest more of its resources in strengthening the K-12 education.

"A lot of the talk about college persistence is about, How do we build the superhuman support to get them to succeed?" Paul Bambrick-Santoyo, who oversees K-12 curriculum for Uncommon, told me during a visit to North Star. "But lost in that narrative is the question, Where are we failing in the preparation we're giving them prior to entering college? Our college persistence numbers are climbing, but I think it's less about what we're doing to support them in college than it is about what we're doing in the K-12 arena."

To improve college success, Uncommon focused on how subjects are taught, raising SAT scores, increasing GPAs, and strengthening the rigor of science classes. There is a college tracking team at North

Star, but it is relatively modest: Two counselors are assigned to that task. That's intentional. "If you have $1 million to spend on boosting college graduation rates, would you spend it on expanding in-college supports or boosting the quality of grades 5-12?" Bambrick asked. For him, the answer is to spend it on grades 5-12.

THAT MAGIC MOMENT: COLLEGE SIGNING DAYS

APRIL 27, 2018, JAVARIS BRINKLEY MEMORIAL GYMNASIUM, GASTON, N.C.

KIPP Gaston co-founder Tammi Sutton at 2018 Senior Signing Day
— *photo by Richard Whitmire*

CHAPTER 6

A jazz band played as 72 graduating seniors from KIPP Gaston College Prep

paired off to promenade through the gym before several hundred students, family, and teachers gathered here. No, this is not graduation; graduation is a far lesser event. This is Senior Signing Day for KIPP Gaston's 10th graduating class. Similar to almost all the big charter networks, senior signing days are "IT" events, proof to everyone that the schools followed through with the promises made to families when they signed up for the admission lotteries: We will get your child accepted into a four-year university.

If you want to know how these charters grew the percentage of their graduates who go on to earn college degrees by a factor ranging from two to five, understanding senior signing day is crucial. Signing days are events that some urban school districts have started copying, which is a good thing. But what gets copied elsewhere, at least from my observations, is a simple mimic that looks more like a party – nothing compared to what happens at places such as KIPP Gaston. What takes place at these charter signing days is more akin to a wedding than a party: It's a reminder of vows made to get here, and a recommitment of vows to be fulfilled in the future. Signing days are a big reason why the major charter networks post superior college success numbers.

The school's very first signing day, for the Class of 2009, is re-membered by co-founder Caleb Dolan as a magical moment. Watching the eyes of the middle school students as the seniors revealed their college choices, Dolan knew that for the first time all students became believers: They truly were part of a college-going culture. "I am not ex-aggerating. When the middle school kids watched the seniors, it was like they were watching superstars."

> 66
> *I am not exaggerating. When the middle school kids watched the seniors, it was like they were watching superstars.*

After the event, the middle school students were asked to write how they envisioned their own signing day. It was clear that every student had thought about how that would play out. "It absolutely trans-formed the way every other student in that campus thought about this process," Dolan remembers. "It shifted from imaginary to like, 'Ooh,

I can be you know like Adryen. I can be like Katrese.' And I just can't overweight that feeling. And its impact."

WHAT IF MAKING IT TO COLLEGE WAS AS BIG AS MAKING IT TO THE PROS?

Today, senior signing days have become commonplace in many traditional high schools, with former first lady Michelle Obama leading the way with her own go to-college campaign, which can be followed at #bettermakeroom. But the movement started at Texas-based YES Prep charter schools. In the opening of the book *The Power of Moments: Why Certain Experiences Have Extraordinary Impact*, authors and brothers Chip and Dan Heath relate an anecdote that best summarizes what their entire book will be about.[1] It starts with YES Prep founder Chris Barbic and YES Prep's college counselor Donald Kamentz sitting in a now-defunct Houston bar, Ernie's on Banks – a name chosen by a Chicago guy who loved Cubs star Ernie Banks and opened a bar on Houston's Banks Street. Here's what happened next, based on a mix of the book and my interviews with Barbic and Kamentz:

It is a chilly October night in 2000 when Barbic and Kamentz stop by Ernie's on the way home. They are drinking Shiner Bocks, munching on Tombstone pizza, and watching ESPN. It's signing day for college athletes, and there's much shouting, applause, and general backslapping from friends and relatives congratulating these athletes on making it to the big time. "Why shouldn't our families experience the same acclaim?" they reasoned. Most are the first in their families to go to college, many of them headed to name-brand universities. This needs celebrating, maybe even more than the athletes needed celebrating. "Our kids were going to declare their own colleges, and nobody was going to make a big deal of it," Kamentz said. "What if we made a big deal of it?"

Thus was born the senior signing day, in June 2001, just three years after Barbic founded the school in Houston, with YES Prep's first 17 graduating seniors and their families cheered on by about 300 younger YES Preppers and the staff. They all fit into a small theater at an adjoining community center. Maybe this wasn't national sports on ESPN, but there was plenty of drama. One by one, they stepped forward to announce where they were headed next year. "My name is Jessica, and I'm going to Rice University!" At that point they would unveil a college T-shirt or wave a college pennant.

There were plenty of tears among the seniors and their families, but the real impact was on the younger students, who carefully watched the emotion and knew their day would come soon. It was a powerful reminder: Study hard and win acceptance to the best college that's affordable. The book's authors cite Mayra Valle, a sixth-grader attending YES Prep's third signing day and her first. "She remembers thinking, 'That could be me. No one in my family has ever gone to college. I want to be on that stage.'"

In 2010, six years later, when Valle graduated, the senior class had grown to 126 and signing day was moved to the basketball arena at Rice University. The keynote speaker was U.S. Education Secretary Arne Duncan, who noted the surroundings. "No basketball game, no football game begins to compare to the magnitude and importance of what happened here today," Duncan told them. "Thank you for inspiring not just your brothers and sisters, not just the underclassmen here, but the entire country."

When Valle's turn came, she stepped onto the stage. "Good afternoon, everybody, my name is Mayra Valle, and this fall I will be attending Connecticut College." As they did with every graduate, the crowd roared its approval.

Today, YES Prep holds its signing ceremony in Houston's massive Toyota Center, where the Houston Rockets play basketball. Write the authors: "Senior Signing Day didn't just happen. Chris Barbic and Donald Kamentz set out to *create* a defining moment for their students. When Mayra Valle and hundreds of other YES Prep graduates walked onto that stage, they stepped into a carefully crafted defining moment that was no less special for having been planned."

The cover to their book is a bottle capturing lightning, which is exactly what Barbic and Kamentz did. Today, every major charter network carries out some variation of college signing day.

GASTON SENIOR SIGNING DAY: 72 SENIORS, $3.5 MILLION, 60 SECONDS OF JOY

Watching the event here in Gaston offers an insight into how the charter networks use these days not to party, not to celebrate, but to reinforce, to create powerful images and memories. Soon after the 72 seniors took their places along the podium, KIPP Gaston co-founder Tammi Sutton stepped up to the microphone. Her first words weren't directed at the graduating seniors. The students she cared most about were the eighth-graders sitting near the front. Those were middle schoolers who would be arriving at the high school next year. They were the graduating senior class of 2022, just as the graduating seniors at this signing day were the college class of 2022.

In breakthrough schools, all classes are referred to by their expected graduation year: the middle schoolers, when they will graduate from high school; the seniors, when they will graduate from college in four years. And in these schools, doing it all in four years is key. These students, who rely almost completely on a long list of scholarships and grants to pay their way through college, can't afford to fall behind the four-year pace. The 72 seniors here drew about $3.5 million in financial aid collectively.

Tammi gave the younger students a long, direct look: "As eighth-graders, just like our seniors, you're making decisions right now that will affect your future choices. Your final grades in eighth grade will determine the courses that you can take in high school. And the hard work and habits that you are forming now are going to be key factors when you're sitting on this stage in just four short years. As you complete those high school enrollment forms and plow through these final weeks of school, think very carefully about the choices you are making. Because they matter. They matter now. And they matter in the future."

Listen carefully, she advised them, to the 60-second college signing speeches, videos, and skits prepared by each of the 72 seniors. "Those 60 seconds are symbolic of hours, days, and years of hard work and commitment ... Our seniors and the nine Prides [each class is known as a Pride] that came before them represent what is possible in public education across the country. While we currently live in a nation where less than 10 percent of students from low-income communities will earn a college degree, we know that that statistic does not have to define your reality. We know that because our alumni have already graduated college at rates five time greater than the national average."

> **"**
>
> *The 72 seniors here drew about $3.5 million in financial aid collectively.*

She was right about that. About 60 percent of KIPP Gaston's founding class, the Pride of 2009, earned four-year degrees within six years of leaving Gaston, an extraordinary outcome. That influx of returning college graduates – plus the teachers arriving here to work in an expanding KIPP network that now includes 140 staffers and 1,900 students in Gaston, Halifax, and Durham – appears to be the sole reason for the sharp rise in the number of college degree-holders in Northampton County. Those degree-holders aren't coming from the paper mills, nor are they wealthy retirees living in Lake Gaston out earning extra degrees.

After Tammi finished her short speech, the 60-second announcements began rolling, clearly what everyone was waiting to see and hear. But at the end, the time when one might expect to hear a party-on message, school leader Kevika Amar stepped up to the podium for a final message. An outsider might think it was a bit rough. Yes, she congratulated everyone, but within her second sentence she moved on to the business at hand. "I can't wait to attend those [college] graduations in 2022. But in a week, all of you will be taking AP exams. You will be continuing to experience what it takes to study for and ace a college final exam. In the next month, you'll be finishing your 10-page research papers and senior projects." Then she paused, smiled, and said, "I don't hear all the excitement in the room about this." Many of the seniors quietly groaned or smiled knowingly.

Most of Amar's talk was about the task ahead, both the immediate exams and papers they face and the longer-term challenge. "While you've put a lot of hard work into earning your college acceptances, getting in is going to feel easy compared to the journey you have ahead. The choices you make in the next two months and the next four years will have a tremendous impact on your ability to be sitting on your college graduation stages four years from now."

As always, the focus was narrow and highly targeted: Never take your eye off the ball of graduating in four years. That's not a message you'd hear from school leaders in middle-class districts, where the students' fates aren't as fragile, aren't as tied to maintaining a minimum grade point average, aren't as dependent on an array of grants and scholarships, each with unique renewal requirements.

COMPELLING TALES FROM THE PRIDE OF 2018

Watching the Pride of 2018 announce their college choices, two things came immediately to mind. First, that every single graduate from this impoverished pocket of North Carolina was headed to a four-year college. And if the past is any indicator, well over half will earn a bachelor's degree within six years. The second observation: Almost all the graduates chose to stay in North Carolina, most likely a reflection of Gaston's rural character, with many of them attending Historically Black Colleges and Universities in their home state. Several students were headed to selective or highly selective universities – several to the University of North Carolina at Chapel Hill, two to Duke University – but the most common universities announced appeared to be Elizabeth City State University, North Carolina A&T, and the University of North Carolina at Greensboro. Those choices align with KIPP's national survey of its alumni, which revealed that its students are more likely to find a "sense of belonging" at historically black colleges.[2]

Modest in numbers, many members of the graduating class chose to use their 60 celebratory seconds to show their homemade videos on a big screen. Others drew on classmates to act out short skits. One of the most popular, based on deafening applause, were the three seniors in the school drumline, who performed a crisp routine and then announced their college choices.

Adonnia Francis has one of the more interesting, and compelling, personal stories at KIPP Gaston. She moved to the U.S. from Jamaica only five years ago, following her mother, who got a job teaching here. Until recently, Francis did not have permanent resident status, which greatly complicated her college search. In the beginning, she lived in Henderson, about a two-hour drive away. And she made that commute for three years – each way. "My mom wanted the best education for me. The public school where I was from, to be honest, was not good at all. Originally, I didn't want to come here, but I got used to it and I love it now." Not only did Francis endure those long drives, she also played center on KIPP Gaston's girls basketball team for four years, meaning late departures. Her mother had to drive two hours to pick her up after basketball, and then return home. "She made a lot of sacrifices, just for me." Only recently did they move to Rocky Mount, a mere 45-minute commute.

When I visited Gaston a month before Signing Day, Adonnia was vacillating between North Carolina's Elon University and the University of North Carolina at Chapel Hill. At that point, Elon had offered her an impressive scholarship and she had yet to hear from other universities. "I want to double major in physics and computer science with a minor in journalism, because I want to write." Her favorite writing is poetry, but she also looks forward to writing school essays – not a sentiment shared by many students. "I absolutely love it."

On Signing Day, Francis announced her final choice: the University of North Carolina. Why not Elon? "I went to visit UNC and realized they had a much better physics program, because it's much bigger. It gives me more opportunities."

Bernard Lee would not describe himself as one of the academic superstars at KIPP Gaston. "When I came here in the ninth grade, it was very bad. I didn't take my school life, and my life in general, seriously." It led him to fail ninth grade, which he had to repeat. KIPP's intense focus on college, an emphasis that was lacking in his previous experience in local district schools, slowly had an impact. "I realized that my decisions in the present affect how life will be in the future." At the end of his senior year, Lee pulled his GPA up to an unweighted 3.1. When I talked to him a month before Signing Day, he was debating between Winston-Salem State University and Guilford College, both in North Carolina, or Regent University in Virginia. What mattered most were the scholarship offers: Lee, one of three siblings, has been raised by a single mother who packs meat into boxes at a Boar's Head facility. On Signing Day, he revealed his choice: Winston-Salem.

Amaya Pearson, who graduated with a weighted 4.1 grade point average, is going to the University of North Carolina at Chapel Hill, hoping to major in biomedical engineering. Why that major? It's what she experienced there during a prospective student visit. "I saw that and told myself, 'This is it. This is what I want to do.'" On Signing Day, her extended family was there to assist in her big announcement. She is the oldest of five children, the remainder brothers, and she is the first in her family to go to college. "It's a really big deal, and I'm really nervous. Although I faced a lot of challenges – grades, sports, babysitting to make money – I got a lot of encouragement from my teachers. I was able to persevere."

Zadaiah Roye is adopted; her biological family lives in the Washington, D.C., area. "For the majority of my life it was just my guardians taking care of me." Only in the past two years has she established contact with her mother. Her adoptive mother lives in nearby Weldon, where she sells appliances at a Lowe's. One of her older cousins went to KIPP Gaston, so her mother was eager to send her there. "She was just ready to get me out of the Weldon public system." Roye found KIPP Gaston "very, very much" harder than the schools she had known. But there are no regrets. Her GPA is a 3.9, she loves the sciences, and she plans on a pre-med major, hoping to become an OB/GYN. When I talked with her a month before Signing Day, she had been accepted to both Duke University and the University of North Carolina at Chapel Hill but was leaning heavily toward Duke. During one of her campus visits there, she stayed with Duke students who were KIPP graduates. "We were talking to actual students you could relate to." The student she stayed with convinced her that coming to Duke was a good idea despite all the wealthy students who would surround her, a student coming on full scholarship. "What she told me was that at some point you have to be comfortable with being uncomfortable." The announcement on Signing Day: Duke.

HOUSTON BUILDS POWERFUL COLLEGE SUCCESS PROGRAM BUT FEW FOLLOW

HOUSTON

Student Truong Nguyen at Houston's César E. Chávez High School,
where he is part of the district's EMERGE program.
— photo by Richard Whitmire

CHAPTER 7

His mom is a nail technician, his father a barber.

Those are the jobs they found here. Truong Nguyen moved to the United States just five years ago, equipped with only the rudimentary English he learned in Vietnam. In middle school, he endured students making fun of his accent. "That was really discouraging for me." He earned mostly C's and D's, partly because he was scared to speak English. Not that he cared that much about his grades anyway. "I don't know why, but at the time I was OK with that." And from middle school he was headed right into César E. Chávez High School, one of the highest-poverty high schools in Houston, a high-poverty district where that distinction means something. Nguyen didn't seem to be college material.

But one day, something snapped in him. "I realized that college was the only way for me to give something back to my parents, because they had sacrificed so much for me. In Vietnam, they had their own stable lives. But then they sacrificed everything they built to move here to start over. That changed my perspective about trying harder in class. So I pushed myself by staying after school and doing tutorials. I would ask my teachers lots of questions." As for being taunted for his accent, Nguyen took a positive tack: "I saw that as a way of knowing there's still a lot of room for [speech] improvement."

Nguyen was just the kind of student to get detected by EMERGE, the counseling program here in Houston aimed at first-generation students who, with some extra help, would have good shots at winning full scholarships to elite universities. He fit all the criteria, from strong PSAT scores to good grades. Offered a chance to sign up, he did, which is where I found him during a 2017 visit after school in the library, with other EMERGE students working on college selection strategies.

Today, Nguyen ranks first in his class of 715 juniors, and he just got accepted as a Yale Young Global Scholar. That's a school Nguyen fell in love with while on an EMERGE-sponsored college tour. "The moment I stepped off the bus, I realized I could see myself here as a student. I really want to come back." His goal is to become a doctor. In studies now famous among educators, economists Caroline Hoxby and Sarah Turner, from Stanford University and the University of Virginia, respectively, found that the majority of high-achieving, low-income students never apply to even a single competitive college. That study might as well have named Nguyen – until EMERGE picked him up.

It's not that the national charter school networks are alone in building college success programs that see students into and through college. A few traditional school districts do the same. Very few. Less than a handful. But there's a clear favorite in this field, and the first to launch those programs: Houston Independent School District. The EMERGE-HISD program now includes about 1,500 students, out of a total high school student population of 50,000. Roughly half of those EMERGE students are still in Houston high schools, the balance being tracked through their college years. A quick report card on their progress: 95 percent of EMERGE students either have earned college degrees or are on track to earn them. More than 80 percent report having a 3.0 grade point average or above, and 87 percent are expected to earn a bachelor's degree in four years.

This program got its launch in a district badly in need of improved college success. A recent Rice University study looked at Houston ISD seniors who started their senior year between 2006 and 2008. The findings:

- For every 100 seniors, only 19 completed a bachelor's degree within six years of leaving high school.

- Hispanic students disproportionately went to community colleges or technical and vocational schools.

- About two-thirds of Hispanic students did not enroll in college in the fall after high school graduation.

Much like the KIPP charter network, EMERGE was launched in 2010 by a Teach for America alum, Rick Cruz, then a fifth-grade school teacher in Houston ISD. Cruz recruited a small group of other sympathetic elementary and middle school teachers, several of them also TFA alums, and proposed a unique college counseling program. "We wanted to create a program that would mirror what private college consultants do for the wealthy, but tailor it to the specific needs of first-generation, low-income students that we had."

The group won permission to pilot the program at a single high school, Chávez, the same school Nguyen attends. "So we wound up giving a series of presentations to the students, asking them to be part of the program. We were cautioned by the administrators at this high school that there wouldn't be much interest, that if we got 10 kids we should consider ourselves lucky."

But 120 students signed up. Cruz and his team focused on the juniors and sophomores, the students they would have time to work with. Their goal was to match these students with the roughly 60 colleges at that time that offered full-ride scholarships to high-poverty students, and take the multiple steps necessary to get their applications in order.

The result ended up surprising everyone, especially the high school administrators there. "We were successful in getting students into schools they had never sent kids to before. In fact, I believe that school had never sent a kid to an out-of-state private college before." A couple of Chávez students went to Tufts University, one went to Dartmouth, another to Oberlin, yet another to MIT. Clearly, there was a need, and it was immediately embraced by then-Houston Superintendent Terry Grier.

"

*Their goal was to match
these students with the
roughly 60 colleges at that
time that offered full-ride
scholarships to high-poverty
students, and take the multiple
steps necessary to get their
applications in order.*

What played out was a hybrid, an in-district program with a $1 million budget that also had a nonprofit arm able to solicit outside donations. In its first year as a full district program in 2013, EMERGE expanded to eight high schools; the second year, it was close to 20 schools. In that second year, Cruz was approached by the huge philanthropy Houston Endowment and asked: How much money would it take to expand? The Endowment liked the answer, and it invested. Its most recent gift, a second round of financing, was $12 million for three years, an amount roughly matched by the district. As a result, EMERGE runs on a $2.5 million annual budget, able to spend about $2,500 per student per year, which covers both college counseling while in high school (and SAT prep, college visits, the EMERGE counselors) and tracking the students while in college. The program's success has allowed it to push beyond helping just the top students to starting to help all students.

Expanding EMERGE into every high school, however, wasn't the slam dunk one might expect. The initial obstacle that had to be overcome was a resistance to what was perceived as elitism. Why start a program that benefits only the top students? Why do our students need to go to top colleges? Some of that resistance came from the very top, said Cruz. "Today, our school board loves EMERGE, and people in the district love it. But that wasn't the original case. You had people saying, 'Well, what about the other students? Why are you only working with a small group of students? Why are those colleges any better than the colleges I went to?' It took a superintendent who was pretty bold saying we're going to dedicate resources to this initiative."

Another serious hurdle to establishing EMERGE: Only three years ago, 28 of Houston's 45 high schools lacked college counselors. At some schools, someone with that title actually functioned more as a test administrator. Although the district took the aggressive step of paying for Naviance, a sophisticated college readiness/placement tracking software that costs school systems about $400,000 a year, the software was useless without anyone to operate it. "Who's going to submit the transcripts that need to be imported to [Naviance]? asked Cruz. "Who's going to train the students? Who's going to push out the information about scholarships? If there's no one there, the product just sits." Today, all the high schools have actual college counselors.

A more important lift for Cruz was changing the attitudes of many of the district's high school leaders, who didn't see many of their students as college material – and certainly saw no reason for them to leave Texas to attend college. Cruz tells the story of one principal who refused to release transcripts for one of her students who wanted to go to Pomona College in California. "She didn't think he was deserving of going to a top college, or that he should go to one. We had to step in and intervene and say, 'That's not up to you.' Ultimately, the student did go to Pomona," said Cruz, and he is doing well there.

When EMERGE started, many of the Houston high schools lacked even a school profile, said Cruz. A school profile contains information needed by college admissions officers, such as demographics, AP offerings, and SAT/ACT scores.

"That's the basic document colleges use to gauge a student in relation to other students. Many of our campuses refused to do it. They just didn't see a need, because for years they had never had a kid apply to a non-local option. And so [EMERGE'S] program manager had to go in and actually do the work for those schools."

That basic task getting done ended up helping all students, not just those in the EMERGE program, say the counselors.

WHY DISTRICTS AREN'T FLOCKING TO HOUSTON TO COPY EMERGE

While New York City school officials visited looking for ideas and San Antonio took some inspiration from Houston while planning to expand its college counseling, to date, only one district, Orange County Public Schools in Orlando, has actually built its college counseling system based on the EMERGE model. A Bill & Melinda Gates Foundation-funded college success collaboration between KIPP and the New York City, Newark, and Miami school districts just got launched. How deeply those districts will commit to data-based college advising remains to be seen.

Beyond that, there's little stirring within K-12 districts. Why?

Trying to get at the answer is critical if school districts are to start "owning" the college success of their alumni. How else to set out on that journey if you don't stop by traditional school districts such as Houston and San Antonio or the most successful charter networks, such as Uncommon Schools, which within a few years is likely to see a college success rate of 70 percent, akin to what students in private schools and wealthy suburban districts experience?

In Houston, part of the answer is leadership, said Cruz. When the program was first launched, there was opposition everywhere. As noted, many said it sounded elitist, while others worried their kids would never survive at highly selective colleges. It was only the determination of then-Superintendent Grier that led to EMERGE's launch and growth. "College readiness was his passion." In hindsight, what Grier did was "kind of crazy," said Cruz. "I was a fifth-grade teacher working with a handful of kids. And he decided to make this program front and center, to make me an assistant superintendent, to give us the resources we needed." That kind of leadership isn't found at many school districts.

Another factor: Houston has a good teacher talent pipeline. It's probably not a coincidence that Houston is the birthplace of two of the nation's top charter school networks, KIPP and YES Prep. It's also home to the nation's most innovative charter/district compact, found in the adjacent Spring Branch ISD (which has now joined in a broader EMERGE collaboration), and also home to Houston ISD, which in 2013 won the prestigious Broad Prize awarded to the district making the most progress closing achievement gaps.

There are still other reasons why more school districts don't take on this task. Only recently has college readiness, and more important, college success, come to the attention of K-12 school leaders. For years, it was assumed that responsibility fell to the alumni, their parents, and the universities they attended. It's only within the past few years, as researchers revealed the dismaying college failure rates of first-generation college-goers, that the attention has turned to K-12 school leaders: Shouldn't they be taking on some of that obligation?

One concern Cruz picks up from small districts, and rural districts, is that they lack the money to take it on. Houston's per-pupil costs for EMERGE, $2,500 per student per year, aren't possible for them. They have no big foundations to step in and pick up half or more of the cost. Cruz's answer: Go after the low-lying fruit. "The program may not have all the components we have, because you may not be as resource-rich. But there's nothing to preclude you from identifying a [college success] champion at each campus and getting them excited about this kind of work. Essentially, that's what we did. The success of EMERGE has little to do with our curriculum. It's not some kind of magical approach. It's a concerted effort to do something with people who believe they can do it and are willing to work really hard to make it happen."

Once the program gets rolling, there's a snowball effect, said Cruz, as colleges get to know the district. And not just the EMERGE students. When the program first began, a college night would draw only a handful of college representatives. "This last year, we had almost 50 college representatives. They're hungry for our students. They know the talent is here. The top schools have tried to increase their socioeconomic diversity, and they've struggled to do so. And now they say, 'Hey, here's this pool of students.'"

COLLEGES SHIFT THEIR PRIORITIES

MEET THE ERIC CLAPTON OF COLLEGE SUCCESS

FRANKLIN & MARSHALL COLLEGE, LANCASTER, PA.

Dan Porterfield with students at Franklin & Marshall College
— *courtesy of Franklin & Marshall*

CHAPTER 8

The campaign to get more first-generation students accepted into colleges has a storied history.

That's what Pell Grants are about. That's what the battles over affirmative action college admissions preferences are about. But only in recent years, fueled by discoveries that the degree-earning success rates for those students was shockingly low, has the campaign pivoted toward pushing up the college graduation rates – not just acceptance rates. In this campaign some notable leaders have emerged. The KIPP founders, Dave Levin and Mike Feinberg, and KIPP CEO Richard Barth stand out for creating a set of practices to ensure that students enroll in colleges where they are likely to succeed and then track them through the process to make sure that happens. The top leaders at Uncommon Schools pioneered ways to reshape the K-12 years to boost the likelihood of college success. Deborah's Bial's Posse Foundation, which sends small groups of first-generation students to college together, as a "posse," was an early innovator, as well as College Track, co-founded by Laurene Powell Jobs, which prepares low-income students for college. Nicole Hurd's more recent College Advising Corps, which sends college advisers to high schools lacking them, is an important contributor.

Among traditional school district leaders, Pedro Martinez at San Antonio ISD stands out for ushering in data-based college advising on a large scale. And former Houston superintendent Terry Grier deserves credit for embracing a far-out idea by then–elementary teacher Rick Cruz to develop a network there to greatly boost the odds that bright, low-income students get admitted into top colleges – and win degrees. Several academics play key roles as well, in particular Caroline Hoxby and Sarah Turner, whose work revealed thousands of high-performing, low-income high school students who deserved better shots at top colleges. A handful of philanthropists help fuel this movement. The Jack Kent Cooke Foundation has long championed this cause, and former New York City mayor Michael Bloomberg in recent years has played a top role in underwriting professional college counselors to assist low-income students in finding their way to colleges where they are likely to succeed. In November 2018, Bloomberg announced that he was giving $1.8 billion to Johns Hopkins University, his alma mater, so that low- and moderate-income students could attend without having to take out loans as part of their financial aid package.

> **"**
>
> *He is trying to engineer a full-blown revolution around getting first-generation students through college with a degree, a revolution on the cusp of success.*

As in most movements, several people emerge as the key passionate leaders, individuals blessed with the rare ability to light up the issue with inspiring rhetoric and prose, all placed in historical context, likely to take the movement from helping a few thousand first-generation college-goers to helping tens of thousands. In this movement one of those people is Dan Porterfield, who first caught everyone's attention on this issue at Georgetown University and then fleshed out a broader vision as president of Franklin & Marshall College in Lancaster, Pennsylvania. Now, as the new president and CEO of the Aspen Institute, he is trying to engineer a full-blown revolution around getting first-generation students through college with a degree, a revolution on the cusp of success.

HEEDING THE LESSONS LEARNED IN BALTIMORE

Understanding why the lanky, soft-spoken Porterfield (who could win an Eric Clapton look-alike contest) has become the most prominent advocate of the college success movement requires some history, starting with his childhood in Baltimore, the son of two teachers who divorced when he was very young. After the divorce, when he was about 8, his mother moved Porterfield and his sister to a row house in a neighborhood that was all working-class white families, with many employed at McCormick Spices or Black & Decker. Porterfield attended nearby Northwood Elementary School. What he noticed quickly was that he was the only child in his neighborhood who went to Northwood, an integrated school that was shifting to mostly African-American students. His white neighbors all went to St. Matthew's, a nearby Catholic school.

Porterfield didn't think too much about it. That was just the way it was. But that all changed when he was about 10 and a black family moved into the neighborhood. "I'm pretty sure it was a doctor and his wife and their two little girls. A lot of people tried to intimidate them into leaving, throwing tomatoes at their house, writing on their sidewalk, calling them names." Except for his mother, who worked during the day and attended college at night, and who befriended them, "starting with welcoming them with a casserole." As a result, some of their white neighbors turned on his mother, writing insults on the sidewalk in front of their house. But his mother never wavered, Porterfield said.

Soon, a lot of black families moved in, with many white families fleeing to all-white neighborhoods. But the Porterfields stayed. "My mom became friends with more of the new families. We had normal friends who played touch football, roller hockey in the streets, just did stuff together. Part of the political education I had growing up was realizing that I had to choose what kind of white person I wanted to be. There were two models, and they were crystal clear. One was my mother, who welcomed new members to the neighborhood. The other were people who tried to make them go away. The people who were resistant to integration were not the way I wanted to be."

And then came the second defining influence. In seventh grade, Porterfield moved to a middle school that, due to overcrowding, had adopted a shift system that would have left Porterfield waiting at school for hours until his mother got back from her night classes. "I experienced what it feels like in a household when a school system has basically said to their parents: 'You're on your own.'" Desperate for an alternative, his mother took him to St. Paul's School, an elite boys school in Baltimore County, and asked for a scholarship – which was granted. Arriving at St. Paul's was an academic shock. Porterfield had no idea how far behind the traditional Baltimore public schools had left him.

"I didn't know what equations were. I didn't know what an outline was. I remember crying at dinner with my mother trying to understand what an outline was. Diagramming sentences was a foreign concept, incredibly scary." What Porterfield learned quickly, and regards as a lifelong lesson, is that it's possible to catch up. His next move was into Loyola Blakefield, a Jesuit high school, and then on to Georgetown University, later becoming a Rhodes Scholar. At Georgetown, both as a professor and later as an administrator, he made his mark by heeding the life lessons he learned in Baltimore, reaching out to help disadvantaged students.

A BOY FROM THE SOUTH BRONX BRINGS CHANGE TO F&M

Donnell Butler seems an unlikely alum of Franklin & Marshall College, a small but distinguished institution which for years enrolled an almost entirely white student body. Butler, who is black, grew up on

Fulton Avenue in the South Bronx. For those unfamiliar with New York City, the South Bronx, at least in the 1970s and '80s, was a national symbol of urban decay, hopelessness, and crime. Even today, the 15th Congressional District, which encompasses the South Bronx, ranks as one of the poorest in the nation.

Butler's experience there differs from many, in part because his mother, who was divorced from his biological father, met a soldier, which meant that Butler got a good dose of highly respected military schools, both in North Carolina and Germany. Later, when he returned to the South Bronx, he showed up in fifth grade at P.S. 132 and wowed everyone with his sky-high test scores in both reading and math. "Nobody had ever scored that high before, so it became kind of a big deal. I got nominated for a program in New York called Prep for Prep, which helped prepare and place me into a private high school in New York."

Not just any private high school – Horace Mann, founded in 1887 and home to many of Manhattan's most elite and wealthy students. Not surprisingly, in his senior year, Butler had several prestigious college options. He was accepted to both Cornell University and the University of Pennsylvania, but he chose Franklin & Marshall. That's where he felt most comfortable on his college tours, meeting many of the top people there. "I needed to pick a place where I could grow and develop and not get lost in the shuffle. I got sold on everything about F&M, about them being the 'Diplomats' [the nickname for the teams there]." So he came to Lancaster, joining a freshman class that had fewer than a handful of black males, and he graduated in 1995 and went on to earn a Ph.D. from Princeton University, while also staying in touch with Franklin & Marshall.

At one point, while sitting in his office at Princeton, where he worked for a public policy research firm, he got a call from F&M's dean of college, who bluntly told him: "We have a problem." It appeared that F&M was about to admit a class of 500 freshman with only five black male students, meaning the college had made no real progress on diversity since Butler's days as an undergrad. Butler offered some advice, and a year later, F&M joined Posse, which pioneered the college success strategy of convincing schools to take small groups of minorities – a posse – that could lean on one another, easing the adjustment to college life, especially on a small, rural Pennsylvania campus where not only were most of the students white, but most came from well-off families.

Then, a few years later, Butler got a call from a friend. Have you seen this Institute for College Access & Success report listing F&M in the top 10 colleges with the least socioeconomically diverse campuses in the country? This time, Butler reached out to F&M leaders with the message: Not a good look.

What happened next was a series of candid conversations among F&M's leadership. The tuition there was high (today, nearly $70,000 with room and board). F&M was among scores of small colleges competing for students from a shrinking pool of families able to pay full freight. How long could that last? And even if that were possible, the campus would lack any racial and socioeconomic diversity, which would further compromise its desirability. The college's board of trustees realized it needed a fresh strategy, and they happened to be selecting a new president. Where could we find someone who could take us to this new vision? They settled on Dan Porterfield, then at Georgetown University, working as a senior vice president for strategic development, a role that included reaching out to first-generation students.

Butler recalls watching that announcement live streamed and thinking, "Hmmm, this could be interesting." About a year later, he got a call from a top F&M dean, asking for recommendations about fleshing out the new vision, especially transforming the career services office into more of a student development office. Good idea, he thought. Then he got another call from the college dean: You know, you really should meet Dan. How about homecoming? OK, said Butler, but I'm only going to be there for a day. What was supposed to be a quick meeting turned into a long one, with Porterfield's staff saying, "Dan, you really have to go." Then Porterfield reached out again, in December of 2011, this time asking to talk with Butler during the college president's two-hour drive from Washington to Lancaster. "We spent the entire time brainstorming. He kept me up past my bedtime. It was about midnight when we got off the phone."

Eventually, Porterfield and other top F&M deans lured Butler back to the campus, hoping to hire him to help carry out the new diversity mission. Butler made the rounds of the top college leaders – This is a really conservative campus. Is everyone really on board with this? – and found himself, at the end of the day, with Porterfield. "Dan pulls out a piece of paper and he basically does what car salesmen do, and he draws the four quadrants of decision-making [what happens if this happens, what happens if this doesn't happen, etc.] and starts walking through it." Basically, Porterfield argued that Butler was the key guy to carry out the campaign to make F&M a more inclusive institution. Even then, knowing how tradition-bound the campus was,

Butler insisted on meeting with at least one trustee who was truly on board. He did, became convinced, and signed on in the summer of 2012. Today, he's a senior associate dean overseeing the planning and analysis of student outcomes.

Together Porterfield and Butler, with the help of many others, began reshaping the campus under what was called the Next Generation Initiative. A blizzard of changes transpired to bring more first-generation students to F&M: partnerships with KIPP and groups such as Posse and College Track, major shifts away from "merit aid" (often used by colleges as a competitive tool to attract top students whose parents can afford to pay more of the expenses) and considerable fundraising to target first-generation students. The result: Five percent of the 2008 freshman class were Pell Grant recipients. Since 2011, that rate has risen to 17 percent or higher. Need-based financial aid for the 2008 class was $5.8 million, climbing to $13 million by the freshman class of 2014.

To offset those investments, F&M increased enrollment (from 2009 to 2011, the enrollment went from 2,100 to 2,300 students) to bring in more revenue and discarded some programs, including paying to send a group of students and a professor to France every year. The college pioneered new programs, such as F&M College Prep for rising high school seniors, where each summer 70 first-generation students, many of them from urban charter schools, come to campus for three weeks of classes and projects. Not all of them end up attending F&M, but they all return with a taste of what college rigor and college culture are like. To ensure a steady influx of college-ready first-generation students, F&M formed alliances with top charter school networks and advocacy groups that help low-income students to and through college.

BEING THE ONLY BLACK PERSON IN CLASS

Tall, thin, and somewhat shy with a formal bearing, Charisma Lambert, an F&M senior, grew up in Newark, where she lost both her parents before the age of 6. She and her brother were brought up by their aunt, who had two children of her own and worked two jobs – driving kids to school and taking care of the elderly and disabled. "And when she got back, she would jump into cooking for us," Lambert says.

Until sixth grade, Lambert attended Newark Public Schools. When she was in fifth grade, one of her teachers left for North Star Academy, making sure Lambert's aunt received a pamphlet about the well-known charter school before she went. They applied, and after a short time on the waiting list, Lambert started school there.

"I was definitely overwhelmed that first week," said Lambert, who wanted to return to her old school. "In the past, I could get away with doing the bare minimum and still passing and not studying. I went to North Star, and it was like, 'I have to study.'" Gradually, however, she grew comfortable with the challenge. By the time she graduated, she had a nearly 4.0 grade point average and several college options, including Franklin & Marshall, which she chose, in part because she attended the three-week College Prep program. And there were other reasons. "My high school had drilled into our heads that liberal arts colleges are the way to go." It's a familiar message at many top charters, where college advisers seek out smaller colleges where their graduates are likely to receive more individual attention, boosting their likelihood of earning degrees.

Despite having gone to the F&M summer program, the freshman-year arrival was a shock. The class of 620 bore little resemblance to the diverse College Prep session. "It was very overwhelming to go to classes for the first day, and the first week, and come back with the realization of, 'Wow, I was the only black person in that class that week.'"

Not until her junior and senior years, when Lambert took on leadership roles in several clubs, did she begin to have much contact with her largely well-off white classmates. And even those exchanges could be strained. Once, during a class discussion about campus turmoil at the University of Missouri, she noticed that she and two other black students were doing all the talking. When the professor pressed the other students to speak up, one white female student replied, "I don't want to say anything wrong." Another student: "I just don't feel like it's my place to speak about this." The left Lambert exasperated. "They should speak up, to say, 'This is how we view things; this is our lived experience.'"

> "
> *It was very overwhelming to go to classes for the first day, and the first week, and come back with the realization of, 'Wow, I was the only black person in that class that week.'*

That said, Lambert realizes her campus is far more diverse than most private, liberal arts colleges. And she also acknowledges the help she got making it through – four separate advisers looking after her, two from North Star and two from F&M. The North Star counselors, who came to the campus once a semester for her first two years, were most helpful, she said, in managing logistical challenges, such as GPAs and staying on track for graduation in four years, and her upper-class student adviser helped with social issues.

In the end, it all worked. Lambert graduated in four years and now works in a KIPP charter school in Baltimore with Teach for America.

'A CHANCE TO LIVE THAT DREAM'

The talent strategy engineered by Porterfield produced some major changes at F&M. The proportion of students eligible for Pell Grants rose sharply. About 23 percent of the class of 2020 are students of color, compared with 11 percent of the class of 2012, says F&M. Amid those shifts, the SAT scores have remained steady, while F&M has become significantly more selective, according to the college. F&M students receiving need-based aid graduate at the same rate as other students, and with matching or higher GPAs, says F&M.

When my interview time with Porterfield expired, and his aides arrived to insist he stay on schedule with his next appointment, I turned off my recorder and started packing up. But Porterfield wasn't finished. He had more to say. He walked me through the personal stories of about a dozen first-generation students who had come to F&M.

"Take Markera Jones," he said, "a first-generation college-goer from Coatesville, Pennsylvania, who went to a segregated school. In ninth grade, she was the only African-American student allowed into an advanced class, and she stepped out of that class, saying she couldn't go if it was to her advantage and to the detriment of others. She went through the mainstream curriculum at Coatesville High School, earned excellent grades, and was encouraged by her advisers to go to a local open access institution with a 10 percent graduation rate. But because she had visited F&M, she chose to come to this campus. Four years later, she went into Teach for America in Memphis and then earned a full scholarship to get a Ph.D. in psychology from the University of Illinois, where she is now."

After running through his long list of success stories, Porterfield wrapped up: "This is what America and education are all about. Giving people from communities a chance to reshape the country and help us have a strong national future, inclusively and creatively together. A chance to live that dream." This is why Porterfield has emerged as one of the most important leaders in the effort to grow college success rates for first-generation students. To Porterfield this is not a cause; it's an American narrative.

Franklin & Marshall is not the only college or university pioneering new ways to not just reach out to first-generation students but ensure they graduate. In the next chapter I'll describe what UCLA is doing with an aggressive program to bring in promising transfer students from California community colleges. What's different about Franklin & Marshall is that it produced a voice for the college success movement – Dan Porterfield.

PULLING TALENTED, LOW-INCOME KIDS INTO TOP COLLEGES

LOS ANGELES

Queen Kwembe at UCLA's summer transfer program
for promising community college students
— photo by Richard Whitmire

Standing outside a lecture hall on a hot August Tuesday here at the University of California,

Los Angeles, Ramses Denis-Romero looks like the UCLA underclassman he longs to be but isn't yet. Denis-Romero was on campus to attend a six-week summer program for community college students aspiring to transfer to a selective four-year university such as UCLA. His story is similar to those of many of the community college students here on this day: Born in California's Central Valley, Denis-Romero is the son of a field worker who, over the years, worked his way up to dishwasher at a restaurant and finally, today, manager of a tire store in Tulare, outside of Fresno. It's a decent job, but Denis-Romero's father has many less well-off relatives in Mexico who depend on his steady income, so there's not a lot of money to spare for his son's college education. That's how Denis-Romero ended up at the College of the Sequoias, a community college in Visalia. He's talented at math and science and aspires to be a doctor, but achieving that dream probably depends on winning a transfer spot within the prestigious University of California system. UCLA, in fact, would be the ultimate dream.

For most of his life, Denis-Romero has felt like he's one step behind. Early in high school he knew little about college, so his lackluster 2.6 grade point average didn't seem to matter. When he finally figured out the importance of college and learned what it took to land a spot there, he signed up for Advanced Placement courses and boosted his GPA. By senior year, he had an A average, but it was too late to improve his overall high school average much. "I feel like I'm always playing a catch-up game against everyone who has always known what they want to do in life."

Denis-Romero's dreams count, but what matters more about these summer programs at UCLA for community college students like him is that they represent the nation's best shot at dramatically increasing the number of low-income students who walk away with four-year degrees.

Community colleges as a solution for turning around low college success rates for low-income minority students? Sounds odd. Anyone taking a hard look at why so many low-income students fail at higher education is tempted to view community colleges as bad actors. When researching The Alumni, I recall sitting down with leaders from L.A.-based Alliance College-Ready Public Schools and being told that well below 10 percent of their alumni who enter local community colleges end up with a bachelor's degree. Just to make sure I heard that correctly, I had them repeat the numbers. But as I made my way around the country to visit other charter school networks, I heard similar grim numbers. Community colleges, I concluded, were pretty much dead ends for any student hoping to end up with a four-year degree.

And California community colleges? Among the worst. In 2017, California's Campaign for College Opportunity released its "Transfer

Maze" report saying it took an average of 6.5 years for a community college transfer student to earn a bachelor's from a University of California campus, seven years from a California State University campus.[1] Additionally, those transfer students pay an extra $36,000 to $38,000 to get their degrees. "It took me longer than it should have to transfer because I was taking all these courses unaware that they weren't transferable to a U.C. system," said one student quoted in the report. Plus, community colleges in California, and across the country, are famous for pushing black and Hispanic students into remedial courses that throw them off a degree-earning track.[2]

It wasn't until I came across the American Talent Initiative that I began to see things differently. What Dan Porterfield started doing at Franklin & Marshall College is going national with the initiative, which Porterfield will promote as the new president of the Aspen Institute. Aspen has partnered with Bloomberg Philanthropies and Ithaka S+R, a higher education consulting firm, to run the program. The goal: graduate an additional 50,000 lower-income students at some 290 colleges and universities with excellent college success records – those that consistently graduate at least 70 percent of their students in six years. Closely connected to the effort is Bloomberg's CollegePoint, which offers free college counseling to students who lack it.

The initiative focuses on a lot more than community college transfers, but the community college transfer system might be one of its most promising ideas. To explain why, Josh Wyner, who runs the College Excellence Program at the Aspen Institute, points to the "Hoxby kids," the now well-known group of students uncovered by economists Caroline Hoxby and Sarah Turner, from Stanford University and the

University of Virginia, respectively. They found that the majority of high-achieving, low-income students never apply to even a single competitive college.

There are approximately 12,500 high school students each year with a grade point average above 3.7 and high test scores who are "mismatched" every year, applying to colleges well beneath their potential. Those students, the "Hoxby kids," have since been targeted by top colleges and universities trying to make amends. But in fact, there's a bigger potential change afoot from promising community college students. "There are 15,000 graduating community college students every year with a 3.7 GPA," said Wyner, "and they're not just mismatched; they're not matched at all. They're not going to a four-year college." Find a way to pull those talented students into top colleges, the places likely to ensure they will come away with bachelor's degrees, and suddenly you have a surge in the number of low-income minority students winning degrees. You have *The B.A. Breakthrough.*

ELITE UCLA EMBRACES COMMUNITY COLLEGE TRANSFERS

The champion of transfers here at UCLA is a ponytailed, earring-wearing experienced educator, Alfred Herrera, who spent 18 years in the undergraduate admissions department before founding the Center for Community College Partnerships. What started out small has grown to the point where the partnership now runs 11 programs, ranging from one day to six weeks, and in the summer of 2018 was serving 700 students. At UCLA, they learn the ins and outs of transferring, get a taste of college academics and, while staying in college dorms, a feel for what life could be like from inside a prestigious university. In addition, UCLA has developed partnerships with four local community colleges focused on increasing access to four-year universities, and will be expanding to other community colleges in the near future. These partnerships are focused at all levels – administrative, faculty, staff, and students – and are aimed at creating strong transfer programs to open the pipeline for deserving students.

Community colleges, says Herrera, are an important conduit for students, "particularly when you look at students who don't have equal access to college prep. So, if we're looking for students to come from inner city schools, students who don't have the preparation they need to figure out how to get to a university, this is a good way." Herrera gets plenty of support from UCLA chancellor Gene Block, who has embraced the American Talent Initiative mission of growing the enrollment of low-income students.

The goal in this community college initiative is to give these promising students a leg up to transfer to a top-run university, part of the University of California system, maybe even UCLA or Berkeley, the premier campuses. Usually, if these community college students transfer, it's to the less prestigious California State University system (Cal State). What's playing out appears to be working: Among students who participate in the summer program, the admittance rate to UCLA is 65 percent. That compares with its overall admittance rate of 25 percent.

What was striking about the students I interviewed, who were part of a STEM group, is that handling the more advanced academics at a place such as UCLA – the concern I was expecting – was the least of their worries. Classwork they get. Juggling chaotic personal lives – that's the real challenge. Take Queen Kwembe as an example. A native of South Africa, she moved to the United States six years ago and graduated from high school in Anaheim, California. She tried Hawaii Pacific University but transferred to a California community college, Cyprus College, after just one year, in part for financial reasons and partly because she wasn't sure what to study. "I didn't want to waste the time and money."

Kwembe told me what the others said, in different words. In high school, they didn't know one college from another. Just like Denis-Romero, Kwembe feels she was always playing catch-up. "One thing about being a first-generation student is that every lesson learned is learned the hardest way possible. It's like you hit a bunch of brick walls before you realize that the door is right over there. It's like trying to find your way in a dark room." Now, however, she gets it: Going to a top university, she realizes, is her best pathway to a bright future.

The biggest impediment she faces? Not academics, but family issues. Kwembe and her sister help support both her father and an unstable brother. Home, she says with a deadpan voice, "is not a conducive learning environment." Looking at the lives of some of her friends who come from two-parent households with few financial problems, such stability seems a world away. "Having to pay rent and focus on school and what you want to achieve is challenging."

Another student there that day

> "
> One thing about being a first-generation student is that every lesson learned is learned the hardest way possible.

was Estrella Rodriguez. She grew up in Cudahy, a small, very high-poverty city in Los Angeles County. Her father died when she was 13. "There was a lot of gang violence in my community, which was distracting, but after high school I went to Cal State L.A. for one year. I had no mentoring; I didn't know what classes to take. I was just lost."

So Rodriguez dropped out of college and began working at a donut shop. "The next thing I knew, I was pregnant, and that really motivated me to go back to school. So I entered a program for youth who are at risk, and they helped me go back to school, at East Los Angeles College." She was pregnant the first semester and still earned straight A's. Her daughter was born in the fall of 2014. Then came a downward turn, with domestic violence issues, and she dropped one class and suffered from depression.

"Everything has been challenging, because I'm not sure if my mental health will affect where I'm going, or whether it will even be possible." Then she found the Center for Community College Partnerships and won a spot at a four-day program for aspiring STEM students. Her goal is to one day get a degree in microbiology.

As with the other students, her most daunting challenges are personal, not academic. "I've never had a stable home, always bounced around, renting rooms here and there. Being financially stable is a big problem for me because I don't have any support from anybody. My mom is a widow and can't work. It's really hard for me to just rely on scholarships and financial aid that I receive. It's so little. That's really hard."

Paulina Palomino, who directs the transfer center at East Los Angeles College, a two-year college that is nearly entirely Hispanic and is one of UCLA's close partners in the program, said survival is the most pressing concern of students and their families. "That's what it is, survival. Every family here is an integral part to the family's survival. Senior members of the family may need caring for; it's a variety of things. And it's very common for the students themselves to be the voice of the family in navigating different institutions, especially medical care. They know the language, and family members depend on their presence."

Students who transfer to a university outside their neighborhood, such as a University of California campus in San Francisco, Merced, or Riverside, are considered lost to the family's fragile existence. The result: students are more likely to transfer locally, probably to a Cal State campus, despite that diminishing their odds of earning a degree. "We have conferences where we bring the parents in and tell them how important it is to support their child through their journey so they will be successful," Palomino said. This is a national problem, not just a California problem.

WHY SELECTIVE COLLEGES LOOK DOWN ON TRANSFER STUDENTS

So if bumping up community college transfers to a top-tier university looks like a silver bullet, why isn't it being done? Just to put things into perspective, at highly selective colleges and universities, transfers, especially from lightly regarded community colleges, are not common. In a much publicized move in the spring of 2018, Princeton University announced it had just accepted its first transfer students since a moratorium on transfers began in 1990. The elite university gave itself a pat on the back and issued this statement, which made me think of a favorite professor who always described such utterances as "penetrating glimpses into the obvious"[3]: "Experience at other universities shows that transfer programs can provide a vehicle to attract students with diverse backgrounds and experiences, such as qualified military veterans and students from low-income backgrounds, including some who might begin their careers at community colleges." True enough, but why so little so late?

The number of transfers Princeton settled on: 13. The number of community college transfer students UCLA accepts every year: roughly 4,000. Of those, about 3,000 enroll. What's happening here, which is a rarity, just doesn't happen elsewhere at this scale, not even at the fellow elite UC Berkeley. Why?

Here's the rather obvious "secret" why colleges and universities for decades performed miserably with first-generation students, admitting too few and doing far too little to ensure their success. It's because colleges are conditioned to exclude, not include, students. "Status is more and more based on how many people you don't serve," Scott Ralls, president of Northern Virginia Community College (who in the spring of 2019 took a new job as president of a community college in North Carolina), told a gathering at the Aspen Institute. Exclusion, which requires building up massive numbers of applicants and admitting few, makes them look highly selective. That, in turn, draws in top-scoring students, who boost the colleges' standing on rankings such as the U.S. News & World Report listings – not to mention their bottom line, given that those same students are likely to come from wealthy families who can afford to pony up full tuition, and make those wonderful donations to boot.

There are other reasons why selective colleges and universities look down on transfers. Elite universities like to think they "build" their students from the ground up, meaning you're not really a Harvard or a Princeton graduate unless you start there your freshman year. And even if some transfer students are allowed, those from community colleges are generally spurned. I mean, aren't community college students there because they muffed high school? At a conference I attended at the Aspen Institute in Washington about community college transfers, I heard one higher education expert refer to it as the "private college disease."

Private colleges, however, are not the only exclusivity snobs. At that same conference, I heard George Mason University president Ángel Cabrera talk about the resistance he ran across while trying to expand his school's community college transfers. Many of the professors and administrators at Mason, he said, wanted to push Mason more in the direction of the elite University of Virginia, which, like most top public universities, basks in the aura of exclusivity. Aligning more with Northern Virginia Community College, he was advised, was moving the other way. It was never uttered directly out loud, he said, but it was the "unspoken tone" of many conversations. Cabrera ignored their advice and instead tapped the accelerator on transfers.

A BREAKTHROUGH MODEL IN NORTHERN VIRGINIA

For years, UCLA has been the national leader in promoting transfers to a four-year university. In the fall of 2018, however, a partnership launched in the sprawling Virginia suburbs of Washington, D.C., that in years to come is likely to match and perhaps exceed what UCLA does. The two players are Northern Virginia Community College (NOVA), one of the largest and most respected two-year colleges in the country, and George Mason, one of the country's fastest-growing universities. For years, the two have cooperated on transfers: Each year, roughly 3,000 NOVA students transfer to Mason, and those transfers have a remarkable success record: Within four years of arriving at Mason, 74 percent of those transfers earn bachelor's degrees, slightly above the success rate for freshmen entering Mason, which is measured at the six-year mark.

Good, but not good enough, concluded NOVA president Ralls and Mason president Cabrera. The two presidents are close. On the first day his appointment was announced, Ralls got a call from Cabrera, and the two have breakfast together monthly. What got launched was a new initiative, called Advance, that works like this: An incoming NOVA freshman declares a major (let's use cybersecurity as an example; currently, 21 majors are options) and then is assigned a "success coach," trained by both NOVA and Mason, who lays out a pathway that guarantees that essential courses are taken, both courses related to cybersecurity and the required general education courses. That gets around the huge problem of community college students taking courses that don't get accepted when they transfer to a four-year university – a waste of money these students don't have. At the end of the two years at NOVA, that same success coach guides the student at Mason, putting them on track to graduate in four years, assuming they attend college full time. The savings to the student by starting out at NOVA is significant: about $16,000, or 30 percent of the overall tuition bill.

The first 129 Advance students started in the fall of 2018. By the year 2023, the most conservative estimate holds that 8,000 students will be in the program. But Michelle Marks, who oversees Advance, believes the numbers will be far larger, perhaps in the 30 to 50 percent range of all of NOVA's 75,000 students. Why? Because NOVA students have every incentive to sign up. Why wouldn't they?

The reasons to expand transfers, Cabrera told the Aspen Institute gathering, go beyond trying to reverse social inequities. It's what the major employers in Northern Virginia want, he said, pointing to the presence of both the CEO and president of Northrop Grumman, a global aerospace and defense technology company, at the press event announcing Advance. "The top employers of our region are constantly hitting us that we're not producing enough talent. You know, we need 3,000 more cybersecurity folks, so this is a talent solution, and everybody gets that."

Avoiding, and mishandling, transfers, said Marks, is "one of the largest failures in higher education." Among students entering NOVA, 80 percent say they want to earn a bachelor's degree, but only 20 percent actually do. The potential leap in numbers is huge. "We're designing a new kind of program that will be a single institutional experience," said Marks. "It could be a commonwealth model and a national model."

Ralls from NOVA agrees. "For over 20 years, I've worked in community colleges that have helped thousands of students. When I ask why they came here, never has one said, 'When I was a little girl, I dreamed of always having an associate's degree.' They don't come to us for our degrees. They come to us to get to a better place for them and their families, which means they're trying to get to a career where the

"

They don't come to us for our degrees. They come to us to get to a better place for them and their families.

next stop is either the university or into a job ... That's why, for us, when we look at success, we should try to see how many students after six years have a bachelor's degree, not just an associate's degree."

What's already working at UCLA, and launched in Northern Virginia, is a breakthrough model.

Are UCLA, George Mason University, and Northern Virginia Community College alone here? Hardly. The American Talent Initiative has many partners willing to help out in achieving the goal of graduating an additional 50,000 low-income students at the 296 college and universities that currently graduate at least 70 percent of their students within six years. And over three years, the University Innovation Alliance, a national coalition of 11 public research universities with the goal of increasing diversity, says it has boosted the number of low-income graduates by 25 percent, which translates to another 6,000 graduates per year.

The University of Texas at Austin is a notable standout, having committed to improving its once-low graduation rate for high-poverty students.[4] The university uses predictive analytics to identify more than 2,000 first-year students who need extra support. That support program offers financial scholarships, academic counseling, and peer mentoring. It's resulted in a dramatic spike in college success rates, with the percentage of first-generation students graduating in four years rising from 41 percent in 2012 to 61.5 percent in 2018.

By creating programs that track students in trouble and offer grants for miscellaneous expenses, Georgia State University is yet another pioneer in making college work for low-income students.

FIGHTING THE ISOLATION OF FIRST-GENERATION STUDENTS

A striking story from researching The Alumni series involved a Dartmouth camping trip and was told to my by Yaritza Gonzalez, who was born in California to parents who picked strawberries when she was young and later moved to Inglewood near the LAX airport, where they work as restaurant servers. English was not the first language for many of the people who grew up in Gonzalez's neighborhood, and the schools she attended were heavily Hispanic. But after graduating as salutatorian from a Green Dot charter high school, Gonzalez won a full scholarship to Dartmouth, where she was immediately immersed in a primarily white, privileged culture.

The first shock came after showing up for the traditional outdoor get-to-know-your-classmates adventure at Dartmouth. She ended up on a strenuous hiking trip in the White Mountains of New Hampshire. "I never really hiked before in my life. My parents never really took me or they didn't have time because of work. A lot of my classmates had been Boy Scouts or Girl Scouts. They had done this before, so they were pretty prepared with the equipment, the hiking boots, everything. I had to buy new hiking boots and hadn't been able to break them in. And I had to borrow some equipment from the college, which was kind of broken. So the experience was not the best. I definitely learned a lot and I challenged my mental capacity to just keep going even though I was all the way in the back most of the time."

Whenever she was asked to talk about her background, she found stunned silence among her classmates. "They weren't being mean, they just had no way of relating. Better to say nothing than something inappropriate." In classwork, she had to fight what nearly all first-generation students experience: the lure of isolation, the reluctance to build a campus community, the fear of asking for help. "Many [first-generation] students are intimidated to ask a professor for help or an extension," she said. "We feel like we're being judged, that it would show we're not prepared, that we can't handle the rigor."

Before *The B.A. Breakthrough* reaches a true tipping point, students such as Yaritza Gonzalez have to be fully welcomed at colleges, including on the freshman get-to-know-you backpacking trips. In East Los Angeles, it's an accepted fact that backpacking is not a neighborhood sport. At Dartmouth, this may be considered a revelation.

4

GROWING THE BREAKTHROUGH

THE TACO BELL
PARKING LOT MOMENT

Nicole Hurd (third from left), founder of College Advising Corps, with students headed off to college
— *courtesy of College Advising Corps*

CHAPTER 10

In May 2004, Nicole Hurd walked out of a meeting in Charlottesville, Virginia,

reached her car in the nearby Taco Bell parking lot, and turned to her University of Virginia colleagues, informing them that she had just had an epiphany. Hurd recalls her colleagues looking at her like she was crazy. But with the benefit of hindsight, it really was an epiphany, one that changed her life and the lives of thousands of high school seniors attending schools that offer little in the way of college counseling.

The meeting Hurd attended was organized by the Jack Kent Cooke Foundation, named for the late owner of the Washington Redskins who directed much of his fortune into scholarships and other programs that target first-generation students, especially those high-achieving, low-income students who usually never find their way into the selective colleges where they are most likely to actually earn degrees. One of Hurd's programs at the university was to offer help to students applying for foundation support, which was why she got invited to the meeting.

> "
> *Across Virginia, the counselor-to-student ratio was 1 to 369. And in other parts of the country, it was even more dismal.*

What she heard at that gathering surprised her. Across Virginia, the counselor-to-student ratio was 1 to 369. And in other parts of the country, it was even more dismal. "My jaw hit the ground. I knew it was bad, but there was something about that number that was really obtuse. And that's not even the worst [ratio] in the country." The next slide she saw showed that 79 percent of Virginians graduate from high school on schedule, but only 53 percent of those were going to college. "While I was aware of the gaps in opportunity for all students, there was something about the data I saw that day that my reaction was: 'You have got to be kidding me!'"

All that led to the Taco Bell parking lot epiphany. Hurd had seen scores of UVA graduates head into Teach for America or the Peace Corps. Wouldn't those same idealistic graduates sign up for a college counseling fellowship akin to TFA? That night she wrote an email to her boss at the university: What if we put our recent college graduates into low-income or under-resourced high schools across Virginia and got more students into higher education and, hopefully, complete it? Her boss's response: Let's do it.

When Hurd and her colleagues pitched the foundation for funding, they agreed and she received a $623,000 grant for a two-year pilot for what was then called the College Guide Program. Every national organization starts with small steps, and for Hurd's new organization that step was a road trip. She boarded a bus with the 14 selected recent graduates, visiting all the colleges in the state where students are likely to apply. At first, there was some suspicion. When pulling up to rival Virginia Tech, for example, they ran across the sentiment: Wait, you're from UVA and you expect us to believe that you're going to steer promising students equally, not just to UVA? The data show they did just that, increasing applications to colleges across the commonwealth, many by double digits.

There were multiple reasons for the road trip. Not only did the admissions office get to know the new near-peer advisers ("Add us to your Rolodexes!"– an action that would come in handy in the coming years), but the team was able to get inside to ask the tough questions: What's your college success rate, especially for low-income students, and more specifically, for low-income minority students? Colleges rarely go out of their way to make those figures publicly available, but in this instance, in very personal one-on-one meetings, there was no ducking. Those answers factored into the decisions the advisers and their students would make: If you are low-income and African-American, here are the odds you will earn a degree from this university.

The pilot proved itself worthy, and in 2007, with grants from the Jack Kent Cooke Foundation and the Lumina Foundation for Education, it went national with a new name, College Advising Corps. Now located at the University of North Carolina at Chapel Hill, as of 2018, the corps had more than 700 advisers in 15 states, working in 670 schools. From 2005 to 2016, it served more than 848,000 students in high schools across America.

The corps is not the only player out there trying to improve the quality of college advising. But its history is worth singling out because it's a great example of how to get past the tipping point as a quick start-up. Historically, college advising for these neglected students has been awful. Any intervention, such as the corps, brings swift results, in part because much of what it does qualifies as low-hanging fruit, such as paying attention to a college's graduation rate. A pilot collaboration between KIPP San Antonio and San Antonio ISD produced immediate results: In just one year, having a KIPP counselor placed in one high school doubled the number of seniors at that school going to four-year colleges. Switching to data-driven college counseling, matching students to colleges where they are most likely to earn degrees, is the lowest of the low-hanging fruit.

There are many small entrepreneurs coming into this endeavor, such as the software tracking used by the Dell Scholars Program. The program's mostly black or Hispanic students are 23 percent more likely than their peers to earn a bachelor's degree in four years. Why? In addition to offering financial aid, the students get tracked for additional help they might need, both academic and personal. Do they need day care? Mental health support? Academic advising? "What sets us apart from a lot of other programs, particularly university-based programs, is we focus on what's happening outside of school," said Oscar Sweeten-Lopez, president of college success tools at the Michael & Susan Dell Foundation.

Coming up with new ways of guiding low-income students to and through college is getting a startup feel. Two Columbia University students just designed BestFit, which connects high school students with first-generation students already in college. That not only helps the high school students prepare for the challenges ahead, but also helps them pick the right college.

"Students can get more information about the next phone they want to buy than they can details about where to spend the next two to four years of their life," said Asha Owens, one of the designers. Some programs are city-specific, such as the District of Columbia College Access Program, which pays special attention to the "summer melt" problem of recent high school graduates not showing up for their freshman year of college. Or the Bottom Line in Boston, which provides long-term personalized support for students, starting in their senior year of high school.

"

Students can get more information about the next phone they want to buy than they can details about where to spend the next two to four years of their life.

The College Board has long been a player in bettering the odds that first-generation students will succeed, including its Access to Opportunity program (much of *The Achievable Dream*, a book I co-authored, was about those College Board efforts). Probably the most intriguing, and promising, startup is Oakland, California-based Beyond12, which offers traditional school districts the kind of into-and-through college coaching and tracking that they have never done before.

Every college expert interviewed for this book pointed to improved college advising as the tool most likely to jump-start the college success rates for first-generation students. Forcing universities with poor graduation rates to improve appears to be a task worthy of Sisyphus. But offering students data-driven counseling that allows them to avoid those bad actors? That's doable. The new startups are joining the veterans, such as the Education Trust, which is adept at boosting college success rates for low-income students. The trust's College Results Online offers bare-knuckle advice to students, parents, and counselors on which colleges to pursue – and which to avoid.

And then there are some really major new players. In spring 2018, former New York City mayor Michael Bloomberg announced a $375 million education gift that targets college success rates. Smart money knows where to lay down bets. Said Bloomberg: "As important as college-readiness is, we have to make sure that students who are ready actually attend schools that match their abilities. Think about this: Less than half of one percent of students from the poorest 20 percent of families attends a selective college – even though many have the grades to get in. Or consider this: Only six percent of kids at top colleges come from the poorest families. And over 50 percent of qualified lower-income students don't even apply."

Bloomberg's gift will support the American Talent Initiative and also expand CollegePoint, which offers college guidance to students attending high schools where that's lacking. "Through counseling over the phone, texting, video chat and email, we help them through the application process and work to make sure that they apply to and enroll in the kinds of schools that they have earned the right to attend," said Bloomberg at the announcement. "Already, 40,000 students have participated in CollegePoint. Our goal is for more than half of high-achieving, lower-income students nationally to enroll in top colleges by 2020."

BEING PASSIONATE ABOUT YOUR MISTAKES

From what I observed, what's playing out with these different groups resembles what I saw while reporting *The Founders*. Although there are multiple efforts at improving college counseling – what the charter networks have learned, what College Advising Corps has done, what CollegePoint offers – they don't seem to be stepping on toes, at least for now. What's striking is the amount of strategy-sharing taking place. All the nonprofits have taken the time to observe KIPP Through College, for example, and they have tapped into the best of that program. They all embrace the work of Caroline Hoxby of Stanford University and Sarah Turner of the University of Virginia, the researchers who first exposed the dilemma of low-income, high-performing students who never got a shot at colleges that reflect their abilities. The Hoxby/Turner solutions, first laid out in 2013, get cited like the Bible.[1] Not a single person from this group – from top KIPP officials to Turner, the UVA researcher – believes there's a single bullet to solve the problem. It's a package, with some action steps more achievable than others, as I lay out in the conclusion.

And they continue to learn from their early mistakes, and from the mistakes made in the corrections that followed. When I challenged Hurd, of the College Advising Corps, to come up with examples of important course corrections, she didn't hesitate. Rarely do you find someone so passionate about laying out missteps. Her top three:

Lesson 1: All magic is local.

It's always tempting for a growing endeavor to be a top-down organization, she said. But it doesn't work that way. Performance indicators invented at headquarters play out differently in the group, depending on the city and state. "Magic doesn't happen in the national office in Chapel Hill. Here, we can find trends, figure out the best practices, but the magic is local. I learned you can't go top down. You have to let this percolate up from the advisers, from the schools, from the school partners. We've learned that lesson multiple times."

Lesson 2: It's the parents.

College counselors may think they play the deciding role in determining where students end up in college. Or teachers. Or school friends. But the biggest influencers, for better or worse, are parents. "That may sound obvious, but it took us 10 years to figure this out. We're not helping students; we're helping *families*." Years of surveying and data crunching always lead back to the same conclusion: Students themselves cite their parents as having the most influence, even students whose parents never went to college. And that can be a challenge.

Based on my reporting in The Alumni, Hurd is spot-on, especially in Hispanic communities where families are very tight and jump at opportunities to see their children live at home and commute to college. And for those students brought to the U.S. as children and protected under the now-uncertain Deferred Action for Childhood Arrivals program, going beyond their hometown is especially daunting. It means their parents are unlikely to ever come visit, even on graduation day. That's a tough one for both students and parents to accept.

"The reality is that parents are still influencing their children about college, even if they didn't go themselves, which might explain why we see some resistance or hesitancy. If mom and dad didn't go, they're probably deferring to what they're reading in the newspaper, what they're hearing from their friends, what their co-worker's child did. You know, they're getting incomplete advice, so how could they be giving great advice to their child?"

> "
>
> *The biggest misunderstanding parents have is about affordability.*

The biggest misunderstanding parents have is about affordability. "They say to their child, 'Don't go, we can't afford it. We need you to work.'" What's missing is the broader look at return on investment. "When talking about higher education, we use consumer language rather than investment language. We talk about debt, we talk about how expensive it is, but we don't talk about return on investment" and we need to, she said.

Another thing to keep in mind with these parents, said Hurd, is that communicating means shifting to texting. "I think the charters have had the same experience. If mom and dad are working two or three shifts, or they don't feel comfortable coming to school, or they are undocumented, you have to figure out a way to get information to them where they feel safe, where they feel supported." That can mean going to churches and libraries. But it definitely calls for texting. "It's amazing the penetration of mobile phones in low-income communities. It's sky high."

Lesson 3: Injecting more technology into college advising and tracking is important, but not enough.

Recent technology advances in this field are remarkable, such as the software programs designed by Matt Niksch at the Noble Network of Charter Schools. My favorite new program: Students get to peek not just at which colleges are most likely to accept them and which are most likely to ensure they graduate, but also whether a certain major at the school is likely to pay off in the long run, especially if there's projected student debt. And the beta form of college tracking software is just getting field testing. That means a software program keeps track of all the key steps, such as renewing financial aid forms and signing up for next-semester classes, and sends constant text messages.

All good, said Hurd, but still not enough. "I'm not sure technology will ever get us to the finish line. It will get us close, but not through. There's too much emotion involved. For a first-generation student afraid of leaving home and what that means in terms of your connections to family – that's never going to be answered by an online tutorial. It all comes down to the student hearing four words: I believe in you.

There's a human-capital piece to this, and we are continuing to explore how to address the challenge of scaling human interaction and technology at the same time."

The corps' methodical, trial-and-error approach to college advising, essentially turning it into a science, invites scientific evaluation, which has taken place several times. Allow me to state a brief bottom line from the research: Although it is premature to assess by college completion data, the indicator that matters most, it appears to be working with admittance (between a 3 and 7 percentage point jump, depending on school size, says Stanford University researcher Eric Bettinger, who evaluates the program). It's a promising beginning.

A DISTRICT/ CHARTER COLLEGE COLLABORATION TAKES HOLDS IN TEXAS

SAN ANTONIO, APRIL 2018

Counselor Kassandra Peña with student Edwin Gonzalez at San Antonio's Lanier High School
— photo by Richard Whitmire

CHAPTER 11

In June 2015, when Pedro Martinez was appointed superintendent of San Antonio Independent School District,

everyone in this city assumed he was a good hire. But few realized just how radical that hire would prove to be. Martinez looked around his new district and didn't like what he saw. The students looked just like him, and they were struggling. Martinez's family emigrated from Mexico when he was 5, and he grew up poor in Chicago. He was the first in his family to go to college. What worked for him, going to college, wasn't happening often enough in his new district.

"One of the things I noticed very quickly was the low numbers of students entering colleges, specifically universities. Less than half of our students were attending any type of college after high school, and less than half of those were attending universities," he said. "Most concerning was a mismatch for some of our top kids. I saw our top kids attending community colleges and lower-tier universities." Only about 2 percent of students at the San Antonio district ended up in top-tier colleges or universities.

For years, school leaders in San Antonio had essentially settled, accepting their fate as a high-poverty, low-performing district. Martinez, however, was determined not to settle and set off down an ambitious path to build a "system of great schools" by opening up new, higher-performing school options for parents. That he wasn't afraid to step on toes became clear when he sought out Democracy Prep, a high-performing charter network from the East Coast, to take over a struggling elementary school. Almost immediately, San Antonio rose to the top ranks of innovative districts, joining Indianapolis and Denver.

All the reform moves launched by Martinez boiled down to a single goal: We need more of our students going to colleges, especially top colleges. That caught the eye of Mark Larson, who oversees the KIPP charter schools in San Antonio. As Larson acknowledges, charter schools, including his own at KIPP, don't get everything right. But KIPP has long been a pioneer in boosting college success rates for its low-income, minority graduates. They had this one thing down pat, and they wanted to share. By themselves, they were reaching too few students. Martinez, who seemed open to charters and ran a roughly 50,000-student district, made an ideal collaborator.

Today, neither Martinez nor Larson can recall which of them reached out first, but those meetings happened, mostly at breakfast and lunch. "Part of it was helping him navigate the who's who in San Antonio," said Larson. "I wanted him to be successful." Soon, however, the discussion broadened, and they looked for ways to work together. "We both dream pretty big." The obvious collaboration was college success – it's what Martinez wanted the most for his students and it's the expertise Larson had to share.

Larson took the first step, offering to explore expanding a college success grant KIPP had been promised by Valero Energy Corporation's foundation to include a pilot charter/district collaboration. Larson made his pitch when Valero foundation officials came to visit KIPP. After a school tour, Larson proposed a dramatic change to the promised gift. "I said, 'Hey guys, remember how I asked you for $300,000? I would like to change my ask to $3 million over five years, and let me tell you why.'"

The "why" was this: Larson proposed using a large portion of the grant to run a pilot college success collaboration with Martinez's district. The money would cover the planning work, hiring a full-time KIPP counselor to work in a San Antonio high school, training existing counselors and more. After listening to the pitch, the Valero staff asked to discuss it privately in the hallway. "After two minutes they came back and said, 'We're in. We believe in this. Let's go.'"

What happened next was a surge of collaboration between KIPP college

> *After two minutes they came back and said, 'We're in. We believe in this. Let's go.'*

counselors and San Antonio ISD counselors. To avoid triggering any backlash from district teachers, Larson made sure all the materials got stripped of any KIPP logos. "We wanted our tools to get into the hands of as many students as possible, and we knew that if it said KIPP, some would view it as suspicious, which would have inhibited its use." For the first time, some San Antonio ISD counselors got exposed to data-driven college selection advice as KIPP shared its extensive research on which colleges succeed with first-generation students, and which fail them. That nearby community college your students have been flocking to for years? The odds of them actually earning degrees are slim. Some of the district counselors seemed shocked by the numbers.

At Thomas Jefferson High, the pilot school where a KIPP adviser spent most of her time, counselors estimated that 53 percent of their 2017 graduates were accepted into four-year colleges, compared with only 26 percent in 2016. "We're seeing a marked increase in the number of students who not only are graduating and going to college, but are being accepted to tier-one universities," Martinez said of the pilot. The experiment worked so well, in fact, that in November of 2017, Valero gave San Antonio $8.4 million, a five-year grant that pays for two new college advisers at all seven of the district's comprehensive high schools. Also part of the funding: The district is able to triple the number of students it can send on college tours. And perhaps the less-noticed but possibly most critical part of the gift: The district was able to establish an office that tracks its alumni through college, a rarity for any school system, especially a high-poverty urban one.

The goal by the year 2020 is that 80 percent of San Antonio ISD's graduates will attend college, with half going to four-year colleges and 10 percent enrolling in a tier-one university.

'PEOPLE LIKE YOU DON'T GRADUATE FROM TEXAS A&M'

Lanier High School is San Antonio ISD's highest-poverty high school, where in the past, few graduates made it to prestige colleges. On this day, newly hired counselor Kassandra Pená is meeting with Edwin Gonzalez, a senior headed off to Texas A&M. At Lanier, Gonzalez's admission is considered a coup. But his journey will be precarious as he juggles multiple grants and scholarships.

For Gonzalez, life as a balancing act is nothing new. His parents divorced when he was young; he has never known his father. Gonzalez, who was born in San Antonio, and his two older siblings were raised by their mother, who has a residency permit and works as a cook and dishwasher in a Mexican restaurant. His only shot at going to Texas A&M is with a full ride, which Pená patched together for him. Now she has to make sure he walks that tightrope to hang on to those grants and scholarships.

"In order to keep those grants, you have to submit your FAFSA [Free Application for Federal Student Aid] every year," she reminded him. "You signed up for Project Stay, right?" Gonzalez nods yes. "That's awesome," said Pená, explaining that Project Stay helps students keep on top of their different sources of financial aid. Each has its own renewal deadline, its own academic requirements, and its own rules for the minimum number of course hours that must be taken every semester. Some have community service requirements.

In Peñá, Gonzalez has expert – and very personal – guidance. She grew up in similar circumstances and also went to Texas A&M, where she had to juggle various grants. Peñá also knows what it's like to face overwhelming coursework challenges. She is originally from Chicago, but her family moved to Houston when she started high school. "When we moved, my parents divorced, and it was really tough on my mom because my father had been the sole breadwinner of the family. So my mother started working three minimum-wage jobs to put food on the table for four kids. The only time I even saw my mom was when she was getting ready for work. Then I'd see her asleep on the couch after working a third shift. When I was growing up, I always remember my mom pushing education because when she was younger, she loved school, but her mother forced her to drop out to harvest fruits in the Rio Grande Valley. Peñá's own father, she said, was very traditional. He would tell her: 'You're going to cook, you're going to clean. You're going to learn how to do all those duties.'" Her mother, by contrast, was always trying to pull her away from those chores so she could do schoolwork. "I remember my parents fighting about it, with my mom saying, 'She's going to do her homework.'" For a birthday present one year, her mother gave her multiplication flash cards.

Her mom's academics-first stance won the day. Peñá got a full-ride scholarship to Texas A&M. "My mom really pushed me to pursue a medical degree or become a dentist, so I decided to major in chemistry, even though I didn't do well in chemistry or math in high school." College turned out to be a shocker. She failed both chemistry and calculus.

And when she told her adviser she wanted to switch majors to English – writing was her strong point – her academic adviser said she'd be better off just dropping out. The words that will forever burn in her memory: "People like you don't graduate from Texas A&M."

But Peña believed in herself and registered as an English major without the help of the adviser. Soon, she had a friendlier adviser and got a 3.8 grade point average for the semester. After earning her diploma from A&M, she worked as a college adviser for two years with Advise Texas, a chapter of the College Advising Corps, and then got hired by San Antonio ISD as part of the Valero grant. Her background seems like a perfect fit for Lanier. All the students here remind her of herself. "My goal as a college adviser is to help students not only get accepted into college, but get accepted into a college with significant financial aid so the money burden isn't such a big factor."

Peña also gets something that a counselor coming from a middle-class background might not instinctively understand: Only rarely are students from high schools such as Lanier going to post the kind of college admittance test scores assumed to be needed to qualify for top universities. Gonzalez, for example, has a relatively low SAT score, and his track record with Advanced Placement coursework is not great. But that's no reason to steer students like Gonzalez away from applying to universities such as Texas A&M, places that have what she describes as "holistic" admissions, whereby college admissions officers look beyond just test scores. "They want our kids from San Antonio."

KIPP'S TIPS TO SAN ANTONIO'S COLLEGE COUNSELORS

At a gathering of the district counselors at the Cooper Learning Center, the leadoff speaker is Eduardo Sesatty from the Kipp Through College program. Everyone here knows him as "Lalo," and he's the primary liaison between the district and KIPP for ongoing collaboration efforts. He seems pretty well accepted. Everyone in the room appears to know he just got back from his honeymoon. At this point, there's only a light-touch relationship between the district and KIPP. Sesatty's role in this gathering is to offer "KIPP tips" – practical advice that the district counselors might find valuable. Today, Sesatty has three to pass along, supported by slides.

Tip 1: Sesatty told the counselors that as everyone already knows, there was a major glitch this year with the all-important FAFSA program. In high-poverty school districts, the FAFSA is a dealmaker/dealbreaker process. Without aid, these families, whether from KIPP or San Antonio ISD, couldn't even consider college. In a normal year, maybe a fifth of the students would get selected to endure "verification," a time-consuming process in which the federal government demands extra paperwork – lots of it – to prove the family financial data is accurate. In 2018, however, due to an apparent computer glitch, Sesatty said, about 80 percent of the students got verification notices, a development that was proving to be nightmarish. Parents couldn't understand why they were being asked to provide sensitive financial information from the IRS, which delayed the verification process, which delayed financial award decisions, which, in turn, delayed the college selection process.

It was turning into a disaster. Here's how KIPP is dealing with it, Sesatty said. The students themselves can request the material from the IRS, he explained; all the students need is their parents' Social Security numbers, birth dates, and home address. So KIPP wrote a "script" of exactly what the students should say. "We would pull the students out of class, put them in a room, have them call their parents and read from the script."

Tip 2: The district, Sesatty said, should consider ramping up its college signing day ceremony, which at KIPP San Antonio is known as the College Commitment Ceremony. At KIPP, he said, this is a bigger deal than high school graduation day. "All 3,000 students from KIPP attend," Sesatty told them. "The seniors declare where they will be graduating from college, and they do it in front of all the students. They go up to the microphone and announce: 'I will graduate from Brown University!' By saying when they will *graduate from* college is embedding the idea that this is just the next step. It's not done. They're making a promise to their peers that they will finish this thing.

It's like a glorified pep rally. I call these thing celebratory rituals. You're celebrating that they applied to college, celebrating that they got accepted, and celebrating that they decided where they are going. I showed them a YouTube video from of one of our commitment ceremonies from a few years ago."

Currently, college signings in San Antonio are a citywide event, where students from multiple districts come together. Once there, they gather in groups – everyone going to the University of Texas at San Antonio sits in one section of the stadium. There are no personal declarations, however, no promises to graduate made in front of peers. The district counselors saw the difference, Sesatty said, and wanted to shift to a more purposeful celebration.

Tip 3: For the first time this year, Sesatty said, KIPP came up with a new software tool called a college award analyzer. Once students receive offers from different colleges, they can enter their financial data: tuition, room and board, and also the awards and grants offered to help their families pay for college. "The tool will calculate a return on investment based on the cost of the college, the college's graduation rate, and the potential salary based on what they are choosing for a career. It's a way of seeing college not as cost, but as an investment. Sometimes families may see college and the cost of college as a threat because they don't understand the potential benefits in the long run."

The tool also helps the counselors make the case that choosing a more expensive option often can pay off over the long term. "We can visualize to students and parents which are the better options. Community college may be cheap, but that doesn't always mean that's the best choice."

ANTAGONISM GETS IN THE WAY ... BUT NOT ENTIRELY

So can these collaborations spread? At first, the answer appeared to be unlikely. The KIPP/San Antonio compact started in 2015, proved itself by 2016, and in 2017, the program blossomed with the $8.4 million gift from Valero. That early success, and the injection of outside money, should have looked like catnip to other superintendents: Martinez gets 18 new college counselors for his high schools completely paid for by a foundation, free college advising advice from KIPP, and he gets to watch a rising college success rate for his graduates – all without losing a single student to a charter and getting no resistance from the teachers union. Hard to cast this as anything other than a win-win. So I was taken aback when I asked Martinez how many superintendents had stopped by to see how it all worked so they could duplicate it in their districts. His answer: None.

Why? "I've been doing this work for a long time, and I feel like right now we're at a point where you have this partisan sort of polarized situation where people feel like it's either traditional public schools or charters. If you chose one or the other, the other is the enemy." For most district superintendents, working with a charter amounts to treason, Martinez said. "For me, I see things differently. There are some charter operators that I really admire. At KIPP, I like their dedication to following these children all the way through college, with a college diploma being the goal. At Uncommon Schools in New York, I love the way they measure their success – that these high-poverty children of color can be at the same level as affluent white children."

The issue for district superintendents in places such as San Antonio, he said, is figuring out how to take to scale what the best charters have done with far smaller numbers and with a lot of help from philanthropies. While an $8.4 million grant from Valero was both generous and helpful, that's small compared to what Valero has done with KIPP San Antonio. If the grant were matched on a per-pupil basis, his district would have received $75 million.

Mark Larson at KIPP agrees with Martinez about the charter/district antagonism being a big player in districts avoiding even a win-win program such as the college success collaboration here. But there's another factor, as well, he said. "In education, great ideas don't travel well. We don't like to acknowledge that somebody else has a better idea. In industry, great ideas are stolen all the time. You go out and try to figure how out to borrow it, copy it, or pay for it. Whatever. In the education space, we just don't do that well."

Only four months after my visit to San Antonio there was a surprise announcement from KIPP: A new college counseling collaborative got funded by the Bill & Melinda Gates Foundation that partners the network's national KIPP Through College team with college advisers from New York City, Miami, Newark, and the Aspire charter network in California. In July 2018, I returned to San Antonio (the city was chosen as the meeting ground because of the groundbreaking collaborative here) to observe the initial meeting at a Riverwalk hotel.

On the first day of the three-day conference, KIPP leaders laid out the basics, making clear that their program arose from humble beginnings. In 2011, KIPP discovered that its college success rate was far less than expected. "We were sending 9 out of 10 of our graduates to college, but only 3 out of 10 were graduating," said Sarah Gomez from KIPP Through College. "That was shocking to learn. Our reaction: How could this be happening?" Although that rate was still three times better than the national average for similar students, KIPP concluded it had to do better and launched KIPP Through College, an aggressive attempt to inject science into what had always been treated as art.

A quick summary of what KIPP discovered in those early years.

KIPPsters were applying to too few colleges, when they should be applying to nine. They were applying to too many colleges that had poor graduation results for low-income students. And they weren't applying to many "reach" colleges – a problem because selective and highly selective colleges put far more resources into their students, which pushes the graduation rates into the 90-percent range. "Seventy percent of our students were applying to 'likely' colleges," said Gomez, referring to what are popularly known as safety schools.

The "star" graphic from the entire session, shared repeatedly, showed the graduation rates of colleges that ranked from non-competitive (23 percent) to most competitive (85 percent). But the sweet spot of the graphic, emphasized over and over, was that within each category, such as "competitive," the graduation rates can vary by as much as 20 percentage points. That means picking the right college – let's say within the "competitive" range – can have the same graduation likelihood effect as getting that student into a "highly competitive" college.

So what are the right colleges and the right mix of applications? KIPP pioneered early software programs to build its College Match program, which guides both students and counselors on the path to finding affordable colleges where they are most likely to earn degrees. One of those early software developers, Matt Niksch, left KIPP for Chicago's Noble Network of Charter Schools, where he had access to larger pools of network alumni in colleges. The programs he wrote at Noble were then adopted by KIPP and other charter networks.

The fruit of all that research, including access to the software, is what the partnership offered to these traditional schools. Their representatives seemed especially interested in what the speakers from

San Antonio ISD had to say. That's understandable; they were learning about the experiences of a traditional school district, just like theirs, that was in its second year of a collaboration with KIPP. Linda Vargas-Lew, who oversees San Antonio's new college advisers, described some early payoffs. In just two years, she said, the district doubled the number of graduates headed to selective colleges.

And Vargas-Lew was honest about the reluctance she experienced among some in the district to collaborating with charters. What she heard: "I don't want to work with charters; they steal our kids." Also talking to the group was Ruben Rodriguez, the KIPP San Antonio college counselor who had partnered with the district from the beginning. He described the raised eyebrows among the district's college counselors when they saw the KIPP research about graduation numbers from area colleges, especially the extremely low odds of a student enrolling in one of the several nearby community colleges and then transferring to earn a bachelor's. "When we showed that slide, the reaction was, 'Wait, I've been sending kids to a community college where there's a 3 percent chance they will earn a four-year degree?' We turned it into a social justice issue."

> **"**
>
> *Wait, I've been sending kids to a community college where there's a 3 percent chance they will earn a four-year degree?*

Sharon Krantz, who oversees counseling for Miami-Dade public schools, said the KIPP Through College collaboration began when the district partnered with the charter network to open an elementary school, KIPP Sunrise Academy, in the high-poverty

Liberty City neighborhood. As part of those discussions, the district and KIPP settled on another common interest – introducing KTC experiments in two district high schools in that same neighborhood. Attending the conference were principals and counselors from those high schools. "We want to bring those practices to our district," said Krantz.

Kelly Williams, who oversees counseling at Newark Public Schools, said their counselors do a good job finding spots in colleges. The problem is keeping their students there. That's the part of KTC that she wants to adopt: "That work is very successful under KIPP."

Newark is just beginning to track the college success rates for its graduates, something few districts do. What will they discover? The news may not be encouraging, if a recent Rutgers University study holds up over time. Only 13 percent of Newark graduates end up with either college degrees or professional certificates, according to the study.

Verone Kennedy, who directs charter partnerships for New York City schools, was part of the Empire State delegation there. "My job is to create synergistic relationships between charters and our schools. Our chancellor takes the position that these are all our children; we should not differentiate between the two. How can we be innovative together?"

TEN YEARS LATER, THE PRIDE OF 2009 REUNITES

JULY 2018: ARLINGTON, VA.

Members of KIPP Gaston's Class of 2009 gather in Arlington,
Virginia to plan their 10th anniversary celebration
— photo by Richard Whitmire

CHAPTER 12

The Scene:

A common room at an Arlington apartment building with a view of Washington, D.C. A Southern-themed buffet from Red Clay & Pigs for a small gathering of the KIPP Gaston Class of 2009: shrimp and grits, chicken and waffles, deviled eggs with bacon, slow-cooked spicy green beans, sweet tea.

The mission: These are alumni who volunteered to start initial planning for next year's 10th anniversary. Given that this is KIPP Gaston's founding class, the class that later classes have looked up to since they entered KIPP as fifth-graders, there's a special weight around getting this right. Having the reunion means something more than a mere party. (I wanted to listen to this group's reunion brainstorming, so I agreed to provide food and drinks.)

The attendees: The key organizer is Ashley Copeland, a Duke graduate who works in Washington for Morgan Stanley as a social media adviser (and occasionally waitresses at Founding Farmers, an upscale D.C. restaurant). Also there was Chevon Boone, a University of Pennsylvania graduate, who just left her job as a middle school teacher for KIPP D.C. to join Relay Graduate School of Education in Washington to become a teacher of teachers; Myles Nicholson, a Morehouse College graduate, who works as a data engineer for a company in Baltimore; Jasmine Gee, a graduate of North Carolina A&T State University, who lives in Greensboro and works as a quality engineer for a medical device maker; Devin Robinson, also a graduate of North Carolina A&T State University, who oversees logistics for a health care provider; Sylvia Powell, a graduate of Wake Forest University, who teaches for KIPP at its Halifax, North Carolina, school; Monique Turner, another Wake Forest graduate, who also teaches at the KIPP Halifax school; and Joshua Edwards, a graduate of the University of North Carolina at Chapel Hill, who teaches math to high schoolers at KIPP Gaston.

The moment: Most gathered here are first-generation college-goers, and their stories are complicated. Going to college wasn't something most of their families even dreamed about, until KIPP came into their lives, and made that the goal. Today, however, what KIPP did for them is, at times and for some, an uncomfortable discussion, a moment that calls for introspection. Who doesn't want to believe they would have made it in life on their own, without outside help? And the fact that the KIPP founders are white and they are black adds another level of mostly unspoken awkwardness. Some are blunt, saying they can't imagine what their prospects would have been had their parents not enrolled them in KIPP. Others are more modestly grateful. Two alumni, however, told me they would have made it this far regardless of KIPP. To what extent the Class of 2009 "owes" its successes to KIPP is a sensitive issue on all sides, with KIPP leaders extremely wary of the "white savior" image.

Furthermore, few believe their lives and careers are perfect. Far from it. Being black, and growing up in a place like Gaston, it takes more than KIPP guiding you into college to even out life's inequities that revolve around race, income, family wealth, social capital, and having the right connections. That's something that KIPP is aware of and works on.

> **"**
>
> *Being black, and growing up in a place like Gaston, it takes more than KIPP guiding you into college to even out life's inequities that revolve around race, income, family wealth, social capital, and having the right connections.*

Regardless of all that, there's an acknowledgment, given the reality of what happens to poor African-American students from traditional public schools in that area of North Carolina, that they have "made it." And the scene here, this festive gathering of professionals in a classy party room overlooking Washington, D.C., seems to confirm it.

The discussion: It starts out as small talk, ranging from high school jokes and grudges to inquiries about careers, such as writing software. When the conversation turns to the 10-year reunion, everything gets focused and serious. What about a class gift? Scholarships?

Could the Class of 2009 raise enough money to create meaningful scholarships? What about offering career-and-college mentoring to the Class of 2019? That's something they could do that wouldn't cost much. What about throwing a serious party, maybe getting a member of the board of directors to lend out their house on Lake Gaston? Who would cater it? Would it be possible to land sponsors for their class? Early into that discussion I depart, removing myself as an outside intruder. Later, Ashley Copeland says they concluded the planning by agreeing to produce a spreadsheet laying out their initial plans that would be shared with the entire Class of 2009.

A SCHOOL WHERE SHARECROPPERS' CABINS ONCE STOOD

Recruiting the Pride of 2009 was a leap of faith, on the part of everyone – parents, students, and the two founders. Tammi Sutton and Caleb Dolan had never run a school, and when they were recruiting in rural North Carolina, there was no actual school they could point to. When one finally appeared, it was nothing more than four modular units bolted together. To make it look a little more appealing, they splurged on a brick facade. "Otherwise, people would not have believed it was a real school," said Dolan. They cheaped out on the delivery of the freezer for the school cafeteria, so when the 500-pound unit arrived, they had to unload it themselves. Dolan, his father, and two helpers wrestled it off the truck and into the kitchen. The finishing touch: some grass they tried to grow in front of the school in the red clay that was once a peanut field.

If they were going to make their mark, it was going to be through relentless teaching and successful learning, not through pretty buildings. So at the end of the year, when the first test scores arrived, it was a big moment. Most of these kids, then fifth-graders, had never passed the state test while in their district schools. Would the leap of faith pay off? "I remember going through the kids' scores, which were just numbers, but they were representative of so much hard work," said Sutton. "The fact the scores were above 90 percent in reading and math almost seemed like an anomaly. That just didn't happen. We were like, 'Oh my gosh, oh my gosh, how are we going to tell everyone?' It was a Friday, around 5:30 or 6 p.m., and the kids didn't come back until Monday. So we just got into the car. And it's like crazy, but we first went to our board chair's house. He had a daughter in our first class. Then we just started driving to all our kids' houses. We showed them the score and say, 'Can you believe this? Here's the tremendous growth you made.'"

Soon, it became apparent to both Sutton and Dolan that something more than just good test scores was at stake. "It was really just proving what was possible and wanting to tell families who had believed in this idea, and the kids, that look, this is real. We hadn't just been saying things that weren't true," said Sutton, referring to the promises made to the community.

That was 2002. Much more awaited the Class of 2009. What every student I interviewed cited as KIPP's biggest influence were the class trips that took them out of Gaston and opened their eyes to the world beyond. Dolan's most prominent memory about this class was the trips they took, to Washington, D.C., Boston, and New York. For many of their students, this was discovering a new world. Especially memorable, he said, was the

Boston trip, where they visited Harvard University. The day the KIPP seventh-graders walked through the Common happened to be the same day as the Boston Pride parade. Although KIPP Gaston took pride in its social justice focus, homosexuality had never been broached.

"Unconsciously, we had been avoiding some conversations that might be at odds with our families' and community's values," said Dolan, referring to the conservative social values, heavily influenced by religion, found in Gaston at that time. Dolan and Sutton had a choice: duck the parade or launch into the issue. They chose the latter. "It would have been easy to just keeping walking and tell the kids that we had to get somewhere. But instead the decision was, let's sit and talk and have this conversation. Dolan recalls telling the students, "You can't be just for some people's rights and some people's liberties." Dolan's memory: "Our students rose to the occasion."

Dolan's next most prominent memory: the school's first college signing day, in part because his wife agreed to move to Gaston to be the founding college counselor. "I guess I somewhat owe the Class of 2009 for my marriage." By that year, KIPP Gaston had nearly 800 students in grades 5-12, including its first-ever senior class. Still, however, everything operated pretty much on faith. Would Dolan and Sutton be able to deliver on their promise of college acceptances? Would it all work out? And then the acceptances started rolling in, including to universities such as Duke, Penn, and Chapel Hill. "Those students became like rock stars to the middle school kids. We had them go watch signing day, and it was like they were watching superstars ... We took the middle school kids back to their classrooms and immediately they started writing about what they wanted their signing day to look like.

(At KIPP Gaston, each graduating senior gets one minute to do what they want to announce the college they chose, a skit, video, etc.) For the Class of 2009, commencement followed the signing day. Dolan kept a copy of his commencement address, some of which follows below:

> *Pride of 2009, don't worry I have no advice for you. All my useful advice was used up on the first day of fifth grade. Work hard. Be good. Think. Got that? Cool – all done with the advice.*
>
> *Instead I would like to take this opportunity to share some of what I am grateful for on this very special day.*
>
> *Fifteen years ago Mike Feinberg and Dave Levin founded KIPP for the same reason GCP exists – kids and parents and teachers deserve it. Nine years ago Mike Feinberg left a message on an answering machine (that's how old we are – neither Ms. Sutton nor I owned a cell phone) asking if we wanted to build a school. Without Mike and Dave's courage and commitment to kids this day would not have happened.*
>
> *Our other friends and family from KIPP: In the 8 years since our founding KIPP has grown to serve 16,000 kids. Some of these people you may never have met but they worked tirelessly to help our school and others.*
>
> *I am grateful for the scary, tenuous, traumatic first four years of the school. In a joyous moment like today it's easy to forget*

how hard this was and how far away today seemed even in eighth grade. Standing here it was all worth it.

I am grateful for all of the mistakes the young men and women on this stage made. I know I often didn't behave like I was grateful for your mistakes but whether it was failing a test, smacking your lips, or getting caught kissing on the bus in sixth grade (give a look) each mistake you made ensured that the Prides that followed would have a better school.

I am grateful for each of the 1440 or so mornings I was able to greet you at the buses. Whether you are one of the bright and chipper or the groggy and sullen, seeing you stumble off those noisy, dirty buses reminded me every day that we were all struggling to make this work. It reminded me that you had finished your homework only a few hours before hearing alarms ring, that your moms and dads were hustling you out of bed and signing your planners, how in the words of President Obama's mother "this was no picnic for any of us." This may be the hardest part of next year for me and many of us here I don't really know what it's like to start my day without seeing you guys.

Possible interjection: this speech is really where 2009 takes revenge on me for all the times I made them cry by making me cry like a baby.

I am grateful for Red clay—one of the nastiest substances on the planet, responsible for ruining countless school carpets and pairs of shoes your parents bought. No matter how much grass we plant we will never get rid of the stuff and it will always remind us where and how we began. This school and Pride emerged from a field that used to hold sharecropper's cabins.

I am grateful that one of you will takeover or create the school that ensures everyone who starts in 5th grade commences their college journey in 12th.

I am grateful for the way in which you (the families, teachers, and students of 2009) have shaped children's lives that you may not even know.

MEET THE PRIDE OF 2009

Here are some snapshots of the Pride of 2009, some interviewed in person, others by phone. A fair number of the founding class returned to teach at KIPP, in Gaston or elsewhere. Overall, KIPP Gaston employs 20 of its graduates (out of a staff of 150) as teachers. Said Sutton: "We are thrilled that so many found returning to their communities a worthwhile option and are leading in our classes, our college counseling department, and our offices."

In every class, there are some students everyone seems to know something about. That's Ashley Copeland, for sure. Her classmates know she went to Duke University. They know she owns two properties in the Washington, D.C., area and aspires to own more. They know she's the social butterfly of the class, organizing the organizers planning the class's 10th reunion in 2019. And they know that she's never taken the traditional path, even today, as she holds a 9-to-5 job at the investment bank Morgan Stanley, helping brokers expand their reach via social media platforms, and then for two or three nights a week waitresses at Founding Farmers. "I've always worked two jobs; that's all I know." That was true in high school and college as well. In high school, she waitressed at the Cracker Barrel just off Interstate 95 near Gaston, and during breaks from Duke, she returned to that Cracker Barrel.

Originally raised in Suffolk, Virginia, Copeland and her mother moved to Garysburg, North Carolina (a town near Gaston that's even smaller), when she was 10, a move prompted by her parents getting divorced. Her mother bought a double-wide trailer and parked it on land owned by her grandmother in Garysburg. Unimpressed by the Garysburg schools, her mother was on the lookout for something better and came across a brochure about the new KIPP school starting up. As first, Copeland was hesitant about making a change. "I was already bitter about moving." But she made the move, embraced the intense, college-oriented academic focus drawn up by Tammi Sutton and Caleb Dolan, emerging as an A-average student, accepted by both the University of Pennsylvania and Duke. She started at Penn, didn't like it, and transferred to Duke, which she loved, and from which she graduated (debt free, thanks to grants and scholarships) as a history major.

After graduation, she waitressed at Cracker Barrel for six more months, enough time to buy a car. With that car, she could make weekly drives to Washington, D.C., three hours from Gaston, to search for jobs and a new life. "I knew I was going to work either on Capitol Hill or the White House. There was no other option for me." She started her search on the Hill, going from office to office looking for work. Soon, using a contact from a trip she had made to Egypt while still in high school, she landed a job with then-North Carolina Sen. Kay Hagan. Unable to live in expensive D.C. on just that salary, she began waitressing at Founding Farmers, a job that came in handy when Hagan lost her bid for re-election in 2014. For a year, that was her full-time

"

I knew I was going to work either on Capitol Hill or the White House. There was no other option for me.

job. She loved it. "I earned more money, met amazing people, and had fun. I backpacked in Europe for two months, went skydiving, and saved enough for a down payment for my first home in Dupont Circle."

Copeland has traveled far from her days as a little girl living in a double-wide trailer in rural North Carolina. As the deciding influence, Copeland points to her years at KIPP Gaston, especially fifth grade, when Sutton and Dolan convinced all the students that they would not only go to college but come away with a degree. "I don't think I would be talking to you if it weren't for them. I am blessed and grateful to have had that experience."

Jeffries and her older brother grew up first in tiny Garysburg and later in Roanoke Rapids, a small city near Gaston. Her mother worked in a factory, her father as a custodian. Today, her mother works as a detention officer in a county jail, her father as a custodian in a school in Roanoke Rapids. She first came across Tammi Sutton and Caleb Dolan when they taught her brother during their time at Gaston Middle School. When her brother stayed late at school, she found herself, and her mother, there as well. "They had a great relationship with our family."

When Jeffries was in fourth grade, Sutton and Dolan told the family about a new school they planned to found. Jeffries was ready for something fresh. "I had had a rough year at my old school and thought, 'Wow, school is boring.' I was tired of looking at textbooks. I was ready for something new. I loved Miss Sutton and Mr. Dolan as teachers. I thought they were cool and funny. I was like, 'This is going to be the best, that they will be my teachers.'"

After graduating from KIPP Gaston, Jeffries went on to East Carolina University, where she majored in communications and public relations. After a year working at a county visitor's center trying to figure out her future, she visited her old school and asked Sutton for career advice. They discussed her love of music, and Sutton said they happened to be looking for a middle school music teacher. Preferring to work with smaller children, she ended up as a first-grade teacher at KIPP Gaston. (Her older brother teaches at KIPP Halifax, an expansion school for the Gaston network.)

After two years of teaching, Jeffries decided she needed a change.

"I had this epiphany, thinking, 'Wow, I've never lived outside North Carolina. I want to try something different.'" That something different turned out to be teaching at a KIPP school in Philadelphia, her first big-city experience. "It's like the complete opposite of anything I've ever known. But Philly has this home vibe about it. It's not overwhelming like New York City. In West Philly, I feel like I can wrap my head around it."

Jeffries keeps in touch with many of her classmates, including Ashley Copeland, with whom she talks at least once a week. Her memories of school in Gaston center on how the teachers made learning fun. "I remember in fifth grade learning vocabulary words with Miss Sutton and she turned it into a drama class, where we got to act out the vocabulary words. I loved that. I was learning and having fun at the same time."

TEIA JENKINS

Jenkins grew up in Littleton, North Carolina, a one-stoplight town about 20 minutes outside Gaston, raised by a single mother who worked as a corrections officer. She's unsure how her mother heard about KIPP, but one day she made it clear that a school transfer was happening. No questions asked. Why? Jenkins isn't sure, but she assumes her mother concluded that KIPP offered more opportunities for her daughter. "The school I was going to is well known, but for the wrong reasons."

At first she wasn't happy about attending KIPP, mostly because the long commute meant she had to wake up around 5 a.m. "At that time, I was riding to school with one of my teachers who got there well before school started." What she was learning seemed over her head, at least by the standards of her previous school. But Jenkins eventually settled in, earning mostly A's and B's and entering East Carolina University. "Initially I hated it. Freshman year was like going to high school all over again. I remember skipping classes thinking, 'I already learned this material in high school.'"

But Jenkins persisted and earned a bachelor's degree in industrial distribution and logistics. Her first job was at a FedEx store, followed by a job at a grocery distribution center. Today, she works for Acme United, a distributor of office supplies and other materials, in Rocky Mount.

Jenkins recalls her years in the Class of 2009 with fondness. It was a small world then. Tammi Sutton (whom she still refers to as Miss Sutton, despite the generally accepted practice of alumni, after earning a bachelor's degree, calling her Tammi) was her basketball coach and also taught her English, math, and history. "We were the first class. We were the guinea pigs, so everything we did basically was the first time it was done there. So we created a lot of memories. KIPP definitely gave me a lot of stepping stones."

MONIQUE TURNER

Turner was raised in Roanoke Rapids, just outside Gaston, the daughter of a social worker and a disabled veteran, neither of them college graduates. She was in eighth grade in her neighborhood school when she heard about KIPP. "There was this buzzing about it, with people talking about their kids going to a school that provided college prep. I knew I wasn't being challenged in school, that I wanted something more, so on my own I decided I wanted to apply to KIPP. I brought the information to my parents, and they were completely down with it." So in the ninth grade, she became part of the Class of 2009.

Her transition into KIPP was smooth. "Even though my parents weren't college graduates, they instilled in me very early what I needed to do to be academically successful. By the end of second grade, I could do my times tables and multiplication. I knew what the public school system wasn't providing for me."

Turner graduated near the top of her class and had two prestigious college acceptances, Rice University in Texas and Wake Forest University in her home state. When she won a full-ride scholarship to Wake Forest, the decision got easier. Going to Rice would have meant paying an extra $12,000 a year. "My parents and I negotiated, but they said, 'Look, you don't have to pay anything if you to Wake. So you're going to Wake.'"

Freshman year at Wake, however, was a "complete culture shock." Suddenly, she was surrounded by mostly privileged white students. "I was in class with kids who had been in private school all their lives, who vacation in Prague and Greece, whose parents are lawyers and doctors and judges. It was a humbling experience. Wake Forest taught me what it means when people are able to be successful because of the privileges they have been given."

> **"**
>
> *I knew what the public school system wasn't providing for me.*

Academically, Wake Forest was a struggle, both in the rigor of the classes and Turner's sense of self-esteem. "If I could do it over again, I would have more confidence in myself, believing that I'm capable." Fitting into the social life was difficult as well. "Going to a predominantly white institution made me feel like an outcast, even if that wasn't necessarily the truth. But that was my mindset. So now, at 27, I understand that to be successful our mind has to be in a certain place."

Over time, her college experience improved, especially with opportunities to travel abroad, spending six months in South America, where she was able to bond with a full range of Wake students. "I was able to make connections with individuals that I will have for the rest of my life."

Turner majored in political science and volunteered for Barack Obama's 2012 campaign. After she graduated, Sutton offered her a job teaching at the KIPP Halifax school, which she accepted.

One of Turner's most prominent KIPP memories is of high school graduation, where she gave a speech. "The message that I had in 2009 was to stay connected." And that's what she still does. "We're adults now, and every one of us has our own lives, and we're choosing to start families. When I see my classmates, at the grocery store or at the bank, doing adult things, I always ask how they are doing, whether they are taking care. I want to know where everyone is."

VICTORIA BENNETT

In 2001, Bennett was a fifth-grader at Garysburg Elementary when she heard about the new school. "There was this community buzz about a new school, and I also remember people talking about being afraid that our school would get shut down because it was low-performing, and had been for many years. My mom just kind of came home one day and signed us [her and her brother, Derrick] up and said, 'This is where you are going.'"

Bennett clearly recalls her reaction to the first few days of school: "This is insane." First, she had to start school at KIPP a full two weeks before her friends who stayed in district schools. Then, the principal, Caleb Dolan, insisted on shaking the hand of every student who stepped off the bus. "When it came to my turn, what was running through my head was, 'Why is this man shaking my hand? Is he going to be my principal or my teacher?'"

During those first two weeks, there were no classes, only lessons in learning the KIPP school culture, especially about the school's informal motto, The Pride. "We were told the strength of The Pride is the lion, and the strength of the lion is The Pride." Learning the culture was part of "earning" their classes, they were told.

The oddest part of that orientation, and something every member of the Class of 2009 talks about, was the startling demonstration Dolan and Sutton choreographed to show the importance of "tracking" – following with your eyes the speaker, whether it be the teacher or another student. With all the students assembled in the makeshift cafeteria, Dolan and Sutton suddenly began running around and Dolan leaped through the cafeteria serving window. In hindsight, it wasn't clear to anyone exactly what that was supposed to mean, but it left an impression. "At that moment I realized, 'Oh, man, these people are serious. They are really, really serious.'"

Bennett stuck it out and did well. During her senior year, she was accepted at the University of North Carolina at Chapel Hill and won a full-ride scholarship. Arriving there was rough, however. "It was a culture shock." Unlike Gaston, where she saw the same people every day for 18 years straight, at Chapel Hill, she would go for an entire day and not see a single person she knew. It was the first time she was truly a minority, and the first time she was surrounded by students from well-off families. Once, her study group met in the library and then decided to go out to upscale Ruth's Chris Steak House to get dinner. "I looked up the menu to see the prices, and there were no prices listed ... that's not a good sign." She declined the offer.

Another social impediment: her country dialect. "The biggest thing for me was enunciation, because in the country everything runs together and you don't say full words. You say 'cuz' rather than 'because.' You just say 'fridge' rather than 'refrigerator.' Or 'mote control' rather than 'remote control.'"

There were other minority students at Chapel Hill, but not many from a tiny town in rural North Carolina. When she spoke up in class, she could tell nobody was listening to what she actually said. "Their mouths would drop open and they would look at me like they were in a daze and say, 'Oh my God, your accent is so cute. Could you say that again?'"

Another major challenge from those days: In her senior year, she became pregnant and gave birth to a daughter. "I was the first one [from the Class of 2009] who became pregnant while in college. I remember most people from back home saying, 'OK, you have a baby. You've got to come home to raise that baby.'" Naturally, she turned to her many KIPP mentors for help, but she found their reaction was complicated. "I never

"

Another major challenge from those days: In her senior year, she became pregnant and gave birth to a daughter.

felt like I wasn't supported by KIPP, but I kinda felt like people were hesitant and kind of standoffish when it came to me. They weren't sure how to take it. And today I understand it better than I did back then, because they don't want to make it seem like you're praising and encouraging people to go to college and get pregnant."

Bennett knew that if she came home to raise her daughter, she'd never make it to law school, which was her dream. Encouraging her to stick with her academic ambitions was Tammi Sutton. "She was like a mini-cheerleader in the back of my brain, telling me I could do it. And she was constantly pushing resources to me." The inner voice prevailed. Bennett returned to school and graduated on schedule. After graduation, Bennett went to North Carolina Central Law School, part of the historically black university. That's where she decided to shed her country diction after she noticed it was a problem when applying for internships. "We'd be talking about something and they wouldn't acknowledge anything I said. Then they'd say, 'Are you from New Orleans?'"

She graduated from law school in 2016 and lives in Raleigh, where she negotiates contracts for Advance Auto Parts. "I absolutely love my job." Bennett is the only lawyer to date to emerge from the Class of 2009. She was part of KIPP's first Alumni Leadership Accelerator fellowship program, designed to give first-generation college graduates a tailwind that wealthy students automatically get through family connections in starting their careers.

For Bennett, the program paid off, hugely. At the time she applied for her current job, she lacked the experience Advance was looking for. But after the first Accelerator session in Chicago, sessions with a career counselor taught her how to present herself, how to find connections she didn't realize she had. She found those connections, presented herself perfectly, and won the job.

One more bit of history about Bennett that's important to know: She joined KIPP Gaston's board. "Initially, it was hard to voice my opinion because the people who were on the board were people who had watched me grow up and still viewed me as a kid." But that changed, again with her newfound confidence from coaching that was part of the Accelerator fellowship. "That [coaching] changed the perspective for me. Now, I've taken the approach that it was my school. I know it better than anyone else. Who better to speak to the people in control?"

LOMAR OSBOURNE

Osbourne is a KIPP Gaston alum who seems to have stepped out of central casting and into the role everyone always wanted him to play: college counselor for KIPP students there. But he's also an unlikely player to have made it this far. He's the second of 12 children, raised by his grandmother, in circumstances on which he treads lightly. Says Osbourne: "A lot of things" happened. If students there ever needed a role model, someone who walked a walk probably tougher than their own family life, there's Osbourne, whose path through college was not an easy glide and whose real-life lessons are rooted in rural North

Carolina. What's also interesting about Osbourne is that he didn't even arrive at KIPP – a suggestion from a family friend who was active at the school – until he was in 11th grade. For many teens, that transition could have been rough, but Osbourne said he was accustomed to change. "I just kind of kept my head down and did the work."

At graduation, he had acceptances from several universities, including Chapel Hill and Wake Forest. An offer of a near-full ride at Wake Forest made up his mind, and he graduated from there four years later, with a major in religion and minors in politics and business. While applying for jobs, he also volunteered at KIPP Gaston, helping students who had dropped out of college and needed to be readmitted. The volunteer work went well, and KIPP asked him to apply for a job as a college counselor. He did, and that's where he has been ever since, handling both college advising and teaching the college prep classes, which at KIPP are pretty much the same thing.

Osbourne understands the unique family circumstances experienced by the students at KIPP Gaston. Especially in high-need families, there's always an issue about how far away from home the students should go. The families want them close by, but the colleges with the best graduation rates are often far from Gaston.

Often, Osbourne has to play the "mean counselor" role, beginning with the speech he gives to the departing seniors every year. Going to college, he tells them, requires them to be selfish. Translated, that means sticking to the graduation plan and resisting getting drawn into family issues back home. "A lot of our kids come home because of family emergencies or tragedies, things they feel compelled to be here for. So I'm the mean one, who asks them, 'How much can you really do?'"

Again: Stick to your college graduation plan. That matters. A lot.

Today, Osbourne serves as director of college counseling at KIPP Gaston.

CHEVON BOONE

Boone grew up in Garysburg, the middle of five children in a family that always struggled to make ends meet. Her mother worked in "hospitality," which ranged from motels to nursing homes. Her father was "the community handyman." Later, they both worked at group homes for troubled youth. "From their perspective it's like, 'Hey, we raised five kids successfully together. Let's help raise somebody else's kids.'"

Boone's older siblings attended Gaston Middle School, where they met Tammi Sutton and Caleb Dolan. "They were like the coolest teachers. Growing up, we didn't have steady transportation, so if they would stay after school Mr. Dolan would drive my brother home after track practice or Miss Sutton would drop off my older sister after cheerleading practice. On many nights, my mother would make dinner and they would stay over for dinner. They were pretty much an extension of my family."

So when Sutton and Dolan decided to launch a school, Boone signed up immediately, starting in fifth grade as the future Class of 2009. One of her favorite memories was a dressing down Sutton gave the school, probably when she was in ninth grade, after a series of arguments among students. Sutton gathered everyone in the gym and pulled out some cash. Boone's memory from ninth grade was that

Sutton showed everyone $100, but Sutton assured me it was $10. "Then she gave us a lecture, saying she wasn't in teaching for the money; she was in teaching for us, to better us and help us develop into better humans. So she's talking about it's not for the money while ripping up the bills, one by one, and letting them fall to the floor. She kept ripping the bills while saying we had to work as a team, work in unity, and don't let disagreements hinder us from our goals. But the only thing I vividly remember was her tearing up the money right in front of us. It was pretty dramatic, definitely the talk of the afternoon."

Boone was a mostly A-average student, and she had great college acceptances from which to choose: Duke University, the University of Pennsylvania, Rice University, and Emory University. She chose Penn, which offered a full-ride scholarship, but she found the transition rough. "For the first year and a half, I hated it," said Boone. Most of the students came from high-income families and arrived knowing exactly what professions they intended to pursue. Boone, on the other hand, was unsure about careers and spoke with an accent. "Like, with the first two or three words out of my mouth, there would be times when even the professor would stop me and say, 'Hey, where are you from?'"

She also stood out as a low-income student, a fact that was most noticeable during spring break when the wealthy students headed off for vacation. "They would go all over the place, to California, Canada, Miami, the Caribbean. Some would even travel to Europe over spring break." At best, Boone made it back to North Carolina to see her parents. Back home in Gaston, few knew anything about Penn, even where it was located. Many confused her Ivy League school with Penn State University. But because it was out of state, everyone considered it exotic.

Things got better at Penn for Boone when she joined a theater group and a dance group. "I was able to step out of that quote-unquote 'black bubble' and was able to see the full diversity Penn offered." Most interesting to her was the diversity among the black students. "It was my first time meeting black people who were not African-American. They were coming from Africa or the Caribbean or from a Latin country." As an African-American woman from a small town, she was a minority within a minority.

Boone was also fortunate in landing paid internships while in college, including at the KIPP Foundation and Relay Graduate School of Education. After graduating from Penn, she taught in Newark for Uncommon Schools before taking a job with Valor Academy Middle School, a KIPP school in Washington, D.C. In 2018, she joined Relay in D.C., where she instructs new teachers.

JOSHUA EDWARDS

Edwards grew up in nearby Roanoke Rapids, with his twin brother, Justin, and six other siblings. "Apparently the older you are, the greater the ... chances you will have twins. My mother was 40 when we were born, my dad 44." His father worked for the railroad, sometimes as a cook, other times checking track. His mother mostly stayed at home but later worked in hospice care.

When Edwards was in the eighth grade in a Halifax County middle school, his mother grew worried about recent gang violence. She wanted something new, had heard about the KIPP school, and told the twins they were going. They both enrolled in ninth grade.

"I didn't know what to expect. Miss Sutton led a two-week course where they drilled us on everything we had missed for the last four years. There were some academic pieces, but the main part was school culture: 'If you're going to be part of this school, here's what you need to know. Here's why we exist.' I enjoyed it; it was totally different from what I experienced in Halifax schools." Once classes began, the academic differences became apparent. "At my old school, all I had to do to get A's was to sit down and be quiet. It was pretty simple. At KIPP, you had to work hard for your grades."

Memories of high school? Edwards cites two school pranks he treasures. Once, everyone in a civics/economics class pooled their cell phones, set them on vibrate, and hid them behind the ceiling tiles. Then, drawing on the cooperation of someone in the front office, during the class, the cell phones went off, one after another. "The teacher is looking around and they're starting to buzz like crazy now. He thought it was coming from the ceiling so he took a broom, lifted a panel, and one of the phones fell out. He was confused, but in the end when he found out it was a prank, he wasn't too mad."

The bigger prank was directed at Miss Sutton. The classmates pooled their money, and someone went to UPS and bought bags of packing peanuts. Her car was always unlocked – she often loaned it out to students to run errands, so it wasn't hard to sneak out and fill the entire car with packing peanuts.

In their senior year, Edwards and his twin brother both went to the University of North Carolina at Chapel Hill on full-ride scholarships, and after graduation, they both returned to KIPP to teach, with Joshua teaching math and Justin teaching technology at the middle school. "I had never wanted to be a teacher, but once I graduated, I thought about how I could give back to the community. That was something that Miss Sutton always instilled in us" – one of the reasons why many KIPP Gaston alumni ended up teaching. "I remember her saying all the time, 'It's great for you to go out and get yours and do great things, but what are you going to do to give back?' I started thinking about it personally. I'm an introvert, a really shy person, and so having to teach and be in front of people every day would give me the character skills that I think are necessary. So I figured, why not?"

Has that worked out? "It has. It absolutely has."

CHRIS ESCALANTE

Escalante is important to include among the profiles because while 61 percent of the Class of 2009 won bachelor's degrees, that doesn't mean everyone did. Chris hasn't. College success statistics usually wrap up at the six-year mark, but Escalante's journey represents a good reason to look beyond that time frame. In May, he'll pick up his bachelor's degree, pushing the class success rate up to 63 percent.

One of Escalante's classmates described him as a "hot mess" in high school, a characterization he probably wouldn't disagree with, at least for portions of his life. His father, a native of El Salvador, swam across the Rio Grande River to enter the U.S., met his mom in Maryland, and began a family. But things didn't work out well, for all kinds of reasons, and his mother ended up moving to Gaston, without his father, living in public housing very near the current KIPP Gaston school. Why Gaston? Because it was a really cheap place to live. Escalante didn't meet his father until his sophomore year of college, shortly before his dad was deported back to El Salvador.

As Escalante puts it, his big break in life came when he "failed" second grade in Gaston because he was more interested in dreaming and doodling than schoolwork. "My teachers came to my mother and said I wasn't mature enough for the third grade; that if I did second grade again I might get the daydreaming out of my system." By repeating second grade, he was perfectly positioned several years later to enter the Class of 2009 at KIPP Gaston, which he did, pushed by his mother, who looked at the longer hours at KIPP and concluded this was a good way to keep her son on the right path. "When you're going to school from 9 to 5, you can't get into trouble."

At KIPP, some of the daydreaming persisted, but the intense you're-going-to-college message slowly sank in. "Even if I didn't want to go to college, I mean, it was the only thing I had known. The only field trips I had been on were to colleges." A talented trumpet player and jazz musician, Escalante took advantage of some KIPP-sponsored trips to jazz programs. In the end, he chose Norfolk State University. There, by his own description, he became a textbook case of what happens when a tightly controlled high school student, who was in school every day until 5 p.m., lands on a college campus where classes often conclude at noon. What to do? Escalante held it together for one semester, but by the second semester he fell into the party scene and by the second half of his sophomore year lost his scholarship. "I was out."

Escalante went back home to Gaston, moved in with his

mother, and worked a series of jobs, ranging from a packing job in a peanut factory to stocking shelves at a Food Lion. "My supervisor at Food Lion would say to me, 'You're so smart, why are you working here?'" Eventually, the pressure got to him, and he enrolled in community college to push up his GPA to the point where he could return to a four-year university, North Carolina's Elizabeth City State University, from which he will graduate with a degree in music. His dream job: a high school band director, probably at KIPP.

CONCLUSION: SCALING THE B.A. BREAKTHROUGH FROM KINDERGARTEN TO COLLEGE

Sixth-grader at IDEA Carver College Preparatory in San Antonio, Texas, visualizes what college success looks like
— courtesy of IDEA Carver College Preparatory

In the summer of 2018, I got invited to speak on a panel

at a back-to-school rally in Denver for the entire staff at DSST, the Denver School of Science and Technology. The topic was college success, a new priority at this charter network, and a new priority for charter networks around the country as their alumni ranks grow from a few hundred to thousands. Are they fulfilling their promise to parents to ensure that their children would not only land a spot at a college but emerge with a degree? At that time, DSST was serving 5,700 students in 14 schools; by 2025, the network plans to enroll 10,500 students at 11 campuses. The first part of that pledge, landing their graduates at a college, was definitely a promise fulfilled. The network boasts 100 percent college acceptances for 11 years in a row. Ninety percent of those students choose to enroll. College graduation rate? At the six-year mark, DSST alumni were earning bachelor's degrees at a rate of 50 percent, which is typical among the top charter networks.

Here's what was interesting about that day. DSST founder and CEO Bill Kurtz was embarrassed by that number. He thought a rate that's between three and four times greater for his students than their low-income and minority peers was far too low. Kurtz expects that within a few years that success rate will reach 70 percent – a rate which exceeds that of white middle-class students – and exhorted his staff to make that happen. This is breakthrough stuff. True, the breakthrough rests on three legs: charter networks pioneering new college success tactics, nonprofits stepping up big time with data-based college counseling for all, and colleges themselves realizing they have to do more to make sure their first-generation students walk away with degrees. But the truly surprising development, the element that makes the breakthrough more than a hope, lies in the K-12 years, beginning with the charters and spreading to charter-district collaborations around college success.

What might keep that from happening? On the K-12 side of that question, there are the usual suspects, starting with thousands of schools in poor neighborhoods that don't come close to preparing students for college work, combined with inadequate or nonexistent college counseling that still sends them to the wrong institutions. Now mix in parents fearful of seeing their children leave their hometowns and parents and students who don't understand the risk they take by enrolling in nearby "commuter" colleges that are unlikely to grant them degrees.[1]

Other impediments on the K-12 side? Here's a big one: There's bad – really, really bad – data so that most parents have no idea whether their high schools are graduating students who are prepared to succeed in college.[2] There are school districts that start screening students as early as middle school so that those who don't get past the screenings

– usually black and Hispanic children who attend lower-performing schools – miss opportunities, regardless of their abilities, to attend selective high schools, the kinds of schools that send their graduates to the best colleges.[3] There are "progressive" parents who bought their way into top suburban districts, or private schools, who then shut the door behind them when they vote against opening up more high-performing seats in urban charter schools.[4]

One favorite of mine from the impediment list: the incessant messaging from well-intended education advocates who question the focus on college. Really, they explain, there's no need to send so many students to college. Good-paying jobs as welders and plumbers and electricians await those willing to go through the training. Why take on college debt? [That debate is fleshed out in Chapter 2.] Another challenge: It's common to see a district superintendent arrive on the scene, create great changes, and then, as soon as they leave – and that happens frequently, especially if they are successful – the pendulum swings back and the reforms fade. Will that happen as more districts take on college success as a priority? Of course it will.

There are no easily slain villains in the list above; some of these border on the intractable. Will we ever move away from a K-12 system where quality is based on the value of local real estate? Probably not, because parents moving to those suburbs don't see themselves as beneficiaries of school "choice." They just see that move as playing within the rules of the existing system. Our vast middle and upper-middle class is not likely to throw aside a system that benefits them, so the political clout that resides with them is insurmountable. I saw that in 2016 while reporting on a referendum to increase the number of charter schools, mostly for poor urban students in Boston. But in wealthy suburbs such as Newton, where parents pay close to $2 million for a home that ensures them access to privileged public schools, the voters said no. [For some context, in 2010 Newton opened a new, $200 million high school. Other suburbs outside Boston are opening high schools with price tags close to $300 million.] Despite having no charter schools anywhere near them, Newton voters overwhelmingly rejected the expansion, swayed by the teachers unions that warned that someday charters could threaten their privilege by siphoning off students whose parents believed their children would be better off in charter schools.

The same goes for screened admissions in middle schools and high schools. There is some hope there; in New York City, one of the biggest offenders, social pressure to reduce inequality may be reaching a tipping point, at least in Brooklyn. But if history serves as an example, and it usually does, well-off parents will continue to find more-privileged outlets for their children's education. When it comes to your own children, parents sweep aside societal greater-good arguments and pursue what they think is best for their families. You rarely socially experiment with your own kids. Will there be changes here? Perhaps, but probably too minor to matter.

PROPELLING THE BREAKTHROUGH FOR K-12

Most of the answers are found in the previous chapters: Keep expanding charter/district partnerships around college success and keep supporting innovative groups that spread smart college advising and college persistence strategies, such as the College Advising Corps, Beyond12, the Posse Foundation, College Track, the College & Alumni Program, and CollegePoint.

But there are other answers that warrant more discussion:

Get better data to high school parents

One of the quickest ways to boost college success is also the easiest: Improve the data on the high school level. Just as we saw with the No Child Left Behind law, the real power of the law was in the "shaming" – the fear felt by any school district that got exposed by the data. That exposure, far more than the threat of sanctions, is what drove [modest] improvements. School districts were no longer able to bury their failures by, let's say, giving out schoolwide score averages rather than breaking out scores for low-income and minority students. Eventually, the law had to give way, mostly because it proved to be a giant bluff. Nobody, neither the federal government nor the states nor local districts, had any silver bullets to turn around their failing schools. But the data lesson lives on.

In data there is power. But with college success data, we're in a pre-NCLB state of affairs. High schools don't know – and in many cases would rather not know – anything about how their students fare in college. That's fixable. (See Chapter 2.) "Historically, the data systems between K-12 and higher ed have not been linked and operated independently of each other," said Samantha Brown Olivieri, former chief strategy officer for GreatSchools. "Doing the work of linking data sets is difficult, but it can be done. States are working often with limited resources and competing priorities. They often will report what is required of them by law and don't have the capacity to go above and beyond that." Translation: When states, districts, and high schools want to make those data links happen, they will happen.

One of the most striking conversations I had while researching this book was with Nicole Hurd, founder of the College Advising Corps. When they pitch a high school leader about bringing aboard a corps adviser, Hurd always asks whether they know the college success rate of their alumni. (Hurd always comes in with the real number, calculated with data from the National Student Clearinghouse.) What she hears back is how fantastic their students fare after leaving, with upwards of 90 percent of their alumni going on to college. Then Hurd has to gently break the bad news that many of their alumni never showed up for freshman year, a lot dropped out before their sophomore year, and even fewer ended up with diplomas. In truth, she tells them, your college success rate is half of what you believe it is.

It's all about knowing the data, and nearly all high school leaders operate in a data make-believe world.

Be wary of silver bullets

Just one example of what's being touted as a successful fix: early college, whereby high school students get a leg up on earning a college degree by taking college courses while in high school. It's hard to generalize about the many early college programs across the country; in many instances they appear to be the salvation everyone seems to be promising. KIPP's engagement with Bard Early College in

New Orleans comes to mind. But repeatedly during my interviewing for this book, I came across skeptics. In Houston, for example, the lure of early college was steering students away from the district's EMERGE program [see Chapter 7] that tracks promising students into selective colleges where they are likely to earn a four-year degree. "Sometimes, students are placed in programs of study that don't align with their interests or goals. These programs may not position students to be competitive applicants to selective colleges," said Rick Cruz, who runs EMERGE. "For example, they may not be considered academically rigorous or may fall outside the scope of what colleges are looking for."

In North Carolina, former school leader Kevika Amar at KIPP Gaston High School saw similar problems. "We have this new trend of early college schools in the area that don't have any proven results yet, but are selling a good dream. So I'm actually losing high performers, who think they can go to school for less time and have an associate's degree, although these schools don't seem to be producing associate's degrees yet."

It's not hard to find research touting the advantages of early college, but not all the research on outcomes is positive. One recent study in Texas found that early college had almost no impact on the likelihood a student will actually walk away with a degree.[5] The point of my raising early college here is not to debunk the programs. For many students, these are great choices to both boost academic rigor and earn college credits. The point is to be wary of any silver bullet.

Allow high-performing charters to expand

Nothing has been left untouched by Trumpism, including charter schools. President Donald Trump and Education Secretary Betsy DeVos claim they love charters, which dooms charters in the eyes of many "progressive" voters. That's exactly what happened in the 2018 midterms, which produced both governors and legislatures likely to push for moratoriums on charters.[6] To be clear, the left wing of the Democratic Party started having problems with charter schools even before Trump arrived on the scene. His ascent just made things worse. For many years, charters drew support from both Republicans keen on offering [non-union] alternatives to traditional public education and liberals philosophically on board with offering inner-city kids an alternative to schools that were obviously failing them. The field has now sharply splintered.

The left wing of the Democratic Party [I hesitate to say this, because it's a sensitive issue, but many of them with children ensconced in private schools, suburban schools, exam schools, and magnet schools] has embraced the teachers unions' call to brand charters as a right-wing plot to "privatize" public education. Why not just make all public schools better, they argue. For the sake of argument, let's answer that question: If you really think our long-failing urban districts, which have had decades to turn themselves around, can truly do that, then why are your children in private schools, suburban schools, exam schools, and magnet schools? For low-income black and Hispanic families, who lack the wealth to buy a house in the suburbs and rarely get spots in those exam schools, charter schools offer an important option for parents – an option that, due to changing politics, is under fire in many states.

> *For low-income black and Hispanic families, who lack the wealth to buy a house in the suburbs and rarely get spots in those exam schools, charter schools offer an important option for parents — an option that, due to changing politics, is under fire in many states.*

For the record, I'm the last to argue that all charter schools are always great. I have a long and controversial track record of arguing that charters that do no better than traditional schools in the same district should get their authorizations yanked. To me, the universal maxim holds: Close bad schools, open promising schools, regardless of whether they are charter or traditional district. It's what parents seek, as is clear in cities such as Denver and Indianapolis, where the "portfolio" model of schooling is offered to parents, a mix of traditional, semi-autonomous, and charter schools – a system championed by author David Osborne in his book *Reinventing America's Schools.*[7]

Here's why the political shift disfavoring charters matters: As recent evidence confirms, when it comes to college success track records, the big charter networks, the respected ones, are pulling away from their district counterparts. Based on my research, the college success rates for students in these networks are at least double those of their counterparts, often considerably higher. The recent Rutgers University study on what happens to Newark's students offers an example of what that looks like in one city: Six years after leaving high school, 7 percent of students from Newark's regular high schools earn four-year degrees; 33 percent of its magnet school graduates do the same.[8] Although the Uncommon Schools network was not included in that study, the current college success rate for its North Star graduates from Newark is 54 percent. Based on software tracking current students through the college pipeline, Uncommon predicts that within six years, 70 percent of its graduates will earn four-year degrees within six years of leaving – a rate higher than the national one for students from high-income families. And many of these graduates head off to elite colleges. In New York City, it appears that the top charters send more of their students to top-tier colleges than the vaunted exam schools.[9] The same phenomenon can be seen among DSST graduates in Denver.[10]

That's the problem with letting the anti-charter fervor among left-Democrats continue to build. Assuming that traditional districts continue to copy the college success strategies pioneered by the charters, it puts at risk what appears to be the most effective anti-poverty program this country has ever witnessed.

Target the parents

Stanford education researcher Eric Bettinger has a compelling story to tell about the work he has done evaluating the College Advising Corps. Asked to survey students about where they get their college-going advice, Bettinger found what amounts to the usual suspects: high school teachers, college counselors, coaches, religious leaders, friends, and parents. But then he was able to loop back the next year to find out which of those was the most influential. The results were surprisingly definitive. "The only ones with predictive power were the parents, and that was for both first-generation college-goers and non-first-generation. It was really stunning."

That lines up with my interviewing over the past two years. Regardless of the charter school network I visited, regardless of whether they were serving predominantly Hispanic or African-American students, the message from the college advisers was the same: What we do is important, but it can all be undone by parents. In poor neighborhoods, most of the parents lack college degrees and may be overly wary, looking more at college costs than the benefits a degree can bring. A high school college adviser can lay out all the facts about the value of a college degree, but a parent worried about taking on debt and wanting to see their child stay at home can easily override that, especially during the summer before college. That's a big source of the "summer melt."

The answer is to involve parents early, beginning in their child's junior year. How? In Texas, I watched a YES Prep IMPACT day where top students got to meet the network's college partners. There were as many parents as students at that school cafeteria gathering. Most interesting were the parents of alumni, whose children were in out-of-state colleges, the places likely to offer substantial financing and with graduation rates in the 90 percent range. Their message to the parents with students still in high school was that having your children leave Texas for college isn't as frightening as it might seem. In San Antonio, where San Antonio ISD partnered with the local KIPP network to boost college success, I heard about unique fundraising efforts for college trips out of the region to send not just current students but also select parents, the ones who seemed adept at passing along the word to others.

Learn how to ramp up the adoption curve

Only a year ago there appeared to be no chance of large numbers of traditional districts adopting the college success strategies pioneered by the top charters. But it is starting to happen. [See Chapter 11.] When big school districts such as New York and Miami get on board and commit in a deeper way, others are likely to follow. There are some major players targeting this opportunity. In August 2018, the Bill & Melinda Gates Foundation announced $92 million in grants to 19 school districts, charter organizations, and nonprofits all with the same goal: encouraging more first-generation students to enroll in college and ensuring their success.[11] Early in my research, a leap in the adoption curve seemed improbable. I feared the San Antonio collaboration would go down in history as a one-and-done. Then the broader KIPP collaborative with New York, Miami, and Newark got launched, followed by the Gates grants to a broad range of schools. Actually, it not only can happen; it's already happening.[12]

Keep democratizing higher education

Democratizing higher education, making it accessible to all, means different things to different people. To the founders of IDEA Public Charter Schools in Texas, it means rapid expansion to meet demand from parents and sending nearly all its graduates to college. IDEA is not bothered that so many of its graduates go off to the nearby relatively nonselective University of Texas Rio Grande Valley. Most of their alumni who choose UT Rio Grande Valley come from families that never envisioned their children would be going to college. And for their alumni who got sidetracked from college by "life" and now have jobs and families but still have a thirst for a college degree, IDEA created IDEA University, which allows students to complete degrees on their own schedule. [See Chapter 3.] To IDEA, democratization gets achieved at scale.

Deborah Bial, founder of the Posse Foundation, also aims at growing college graduation success for low-income and minority students, but she embraces a different vision of democratization. Her group operates out of 10 cities and places students [in clusters, so they have a "posse" to help them through] only at colleges that can offer full scholarships. The foundation seeks not scale through numbers of alumni but impact. "Posse's not so much about reaching as many kids as possible. It's about reaching young people who can be strong decision makers out in the workforce. Really strong leaders in the Senate, as superintendents, as principals, as leaders of companies. Clearly, this country needs to focus on leadership because you don't see the demographics of the population reflected in leadership positions in the workforce."

Bial describes Posse as a "tipping point" program focused on changing business and education. But in reality, what Posse does isn't that different from what IDEA does in the Rio Grande Valley. Posse students may end up in more name-brand universities, but some IDEA alumni also win spots in those schools. And in the years to come, the hundreds of IDEA alumni emerging from universities such as UT Rio Grande Valley will form the middle-class backbone of cities in that region, the lawyers, insurance agents, and small-business owners.

Some groups straddle both approaches. KIPP democratizes through expansion, just like IDEA, but also shoots for elite game-changer alumni through its Accelerator leadership program. The Accelerator takes promising alumni, college graduates doing well but in need of the extra edge that upper- income students get through summer internships and family connections, and gives them the networking skills that can accelerate their ambitions. Said KIPP CEO Richard Barth: "Our alums are going to be change agents of the future."

IDEA, Posse, and KIPP are all democratizing higher education, pressuring universities to make room for their students. For universities, that means seeking out students in places they don't normally look, raising money for scholarships, and, most of all, making these students feel comfortable on their campuses. In tracking the college experiences of the KIPP Gaston Class of 2009, I was struck by how out of place they felt at their campuses, except those who went to historically black colleges (a phenomenon picked up by KIPP's recent alumni survey).[13] That affected their grades, their career plans, pretty much everything. Their very presence on campus was fragile, at daily risk.

Nicole Hurd from the College Advising Corps sees the same challenge for the students they support. Recounting recent visits to high schools that organize college signing days [see Chapter 6], Hurd told me: "In all those instances, I saw young people who are afraid that this is not for them. And I understand it. Even the most well-resourced person in the world knows that this is a big transition. And so if there's one thing I could do, it would be make this bridge between K through 12 and higher ed seamless. As you know, there's a real phenomenon called summer melt. I've seen numbers as high as 30 percent of kids during that summer [before their freshman year]. And what scares me half to death is, as I went to those events I could see in the eyes that some of those kids could melt, because in those three summer months, there's not going to be anyone telling them that they can do this. Frankly, there might be somebody telling them, 'You're going to go into debt,'" said Hurd.

If there were another thing Hurd could do, she adds, "So this sounds really, really simplistic in some ways. I would stop the public conversation around higher education not being worth it. It drives me nuts, because the reality is, when you see it on the TV set and you see it on the cover of *USA Today* that student debt is so high, and there's this idea out there that college is not going to be worth it and you're going to end up living in your parents' basement. First of all, that's not true. As you know from the data on economic outcomes and economic mobility, the only way out of poverty is education. The best decision you could ever make is investing in higher education."

If pushing up the college success rates for first-generation students were something easy to do, we'd be doing it already. After all, there has been a surge in the number of first-time college-goers. A promising start, with good intentions all around. It's just that their success rate is awful, despite the clear economic motive to improve that rate: A student who earns a diploma is far more likely to pay back student loans than a student who drops out.[14] And yet the failure rates remain high. Why? It's not that there are hostile forces rising up to limit the number who succeed. There's every reason to believe that Americans generally embrace this as both idealistic and essential to maintaining the American dream. So, what is it?

On the higher ed side, the biggest reason comes down to two factors. First, the elite colleges, the ones where first-generation students are highly likely to earn degrees, with success rates close to 90 percent, are reluctant to back away from nurturing their exclusivity. The more students who apply and the more who get rejected, the more exclusive the college appears in the rankings. Elitism is a habit difficult to shed.[15] Admitting low-income minority students, who may have lower test scores and higher needs for academic and financial aid, could threaten their rankings, which colleges believe drive their recruiting. [Actually, not necessarily. See Chapter 8.] Second, the universities where first-generation students are most likely to end up, the closer-to-home institutions that often qualify as commuter schools, are the places least likely to support first-generation college-goers, which mostly explains why college success rates there are more in the 30 to 40 percent range. The "help" gap extends to public universities in general, which spend $1,000 less on black and Hispanic students than on white students, in part because those students are less likely to end up in the more prestigious flagship campuses, according to the Center for American Progress.[16]

Here's the thing: The higher education world doesn't have to act like that, including the elites. The University of Texas has moved aggressively to boost success rates for first-generation students.[17] And look at UCLA, an exclusive university by anyone's description, where every year the university admits impressive numbers of students from community colleges and dedicates a dorm floor to first-generation students. To UCLA, transfers from community colleges are important to its mission, and important to California. Who ruled that top community college students should only transfer to the less prestigious Cal State university system? The University of California, Riverside, is another top campus with an admirable track record, especially with African-American students. And look at George Mason University in Northern Virginia, which is a respected university on its way up. Already, 3,000 students each year transfer there from Northern Virginia Community College, and a new Advance program aims to grow that number considerably. One of the challenges faced by Mason President Ángel Cabrera in pursuing the Advance program has been overruling internal skeptics worried it could upset their plans to make Mason look more exclusive.

Nor is it written in stone that second- and third-tier universities, the places that draw the most first-generation students, have to do a regrettable job ensuring they walk away with degrees. Georgia State University, for example, ushered in a swarm of changes, some of them small, that drew national attention for proving the university can succeed with low-income students, especially African Americans. The university's early-identification system, for example, seeks out trouble spots such as students missing classes or failing exams, and counsels them back on track. Its Panther Retention Grants serve as the best example of the micro-grants I champion later in this chapter. The impact on college success is striking: From 2002 to 2016, the college's overall graduation rate rose by nearly 20 percentage points and the rate for underrepresented students rose by 23 percentage points. Today, Georgia State ranks first in the nation in the number of degrees awarded to black students.

One non-elite university also using predictive analytics to boost graduation rates is the University of South Florida.[18] The Tampa Bay university claims a six-year graduation rate for Pell Grant students of 68 percent, 1 percent higher than the rate for its students not getting the federal grants for low-income students. Much like at Georgia State, the tweaks made at the University of South Florida ranged from small to large. Veteran higher education analyst Kevin Carey, who profiled the university in The Washington Monthly, offered one:[19]

"USF realized it had been misallocating financial aid. Some students were getting more than they needed, others not enough. The financial aid office redirected aid to students when it made the difference between them enrolling part time or full time, or between studying during the day or holding down a full-time job. Research shows that, as you'd expect, full-time students with room in their schedule for schoolwork are far more likely to graduate on time.

The reforms worked. The percent of freshman who graduated in four years increased from 43 percent for those enrolled in 2009 to nearly 60 percent for those who enrolled in 2013. Impressively, the gains were spread evenly across demographic groups. Slightly more than half of USF's undergraduates are nonwhite, and nearly 40 percent have incomes low enough to qualify for a federal Pell Grant.

Unfortunately, the colleges and universities taking bold steps to increase college success are a distinct minority. Many still focus only on wealthy white school districts for their recruitment efforts.[20] Is it fair to ask colleges to take on all these issues while facing the unprecedented financial headwinds of expenses rising faster than revenues and a stagnant population of traditional college students? Yes, especially considering the hefty endowments controlled by the top colleges and the signs that colleges still don't "get it." What are they doing in the face of these headwinds? Creating more majors to fight over who gets the last of that shrinking population of traditional students.[21]

Again, most of the answers are found in the previous chapters: Embrace the lessons learned from the "democratizing college" movement [see Chapter 3]. Push hard on endeavors such as the American Talent Initiative [see Chapter 9] to open up more seats for first-generation students at top colleges, especially for promising community college graduates. On those campuses, 80 percent of the arriving students say they want a bachelor's degree, but only 14 percent end up with one. Finally, keep supporting innovative groups that spread smart college advising and college persistence strategies, such as the College Advising Corps, Beyond12, the Posse Foundation, College Track, the College & Alumni Program, and CollegePoint [see Chapter 10]. Those are the three legs of "The B.A. Breakthrough." But there are other solutions that either didn't get mentioned before, were only briefly described, or merit repeating:

Make first-generation students feel more comfortable on campuses

There are scores of ways colleges make life tough for first-generation students, most of them unintended. It's just a culture clash. Almost all the Gaston alumni I interviewed cited rough college entries; in some cases they never recovered. Rare was the alum who immediately segued into campus culture; some admit they never broke out of the "black bubble" on campus, even after four years. Craig Robinson, a pioneer with KIPP Through College who now works at the College Advising Corps, has a lifetime of experience in guiding minority students through college. "Getting into college is one of the hurdles, but getting through remains the other hurdle. Higher ed has to think about the culture, and the climate, and the supports necessary for all students to thrive, not just a select few who have parents who have gone to college."

Kevin Carey, who directs education policy at Washington-based New America, says colleges are moving away from their traditional approach of waiting for students to arrive on campus before making services available and believing that if the students don't seek them out, and fail, then perhaps it was meant to be. "Fortunately, they're not thinking that way now. They are doing more deliberate college advising. They're not just passively making resources available. They trying to form relationships. They are trying to make choosing courses more navigable."

Learn the difference between privileged poor and doubly disadvantaged poor

On the surface, "privileged" poor and "doubly disadvantaged" poor may look alike. But they are worlds apart, a fact that many colleges may not recognize.[22] I found ideal examples on a single campus, Franklin & Marshall College in Lancaster, Pennsylvania, where Donnell Butler, who oversees diversity issues there, offered himself up as an example.

"So, there's the privileged poor, who usually come from a major city and had access to some type of college access program or college preparation program or some type of resource that helped them navigate from their impoverished background," said Butler. "So, that's me." Butler grew up on Fulton Avenue in the South Bronx, one of the nation's poorest neighborhoods. While in school, he got nominated for a program in New York called Prep for Prep, which helps prepare promising low-income students for placement in elite private schools. That's where he ended up, at New York's Horace Mann School, home to many of Manhattan's wealthiest and best-educated students. After graduating, he was accepted to both Cornell University and the University of Pennsylvania, but he chose Franklin & Marshall. That's where he felt most comfortable on his college tours. He's the privileged poor.

Now compare Butler's background to that of Mya Jackson, a freshman at F&M. Jackson, also African American and also poor, was raised in rural poverty in remote Gaston, North Carolina. She had no access to Prep for Prep, no prestigious private schools anywhere in sight. She was raised by a single mother who worked as a corrections officer. "We grew up in a really small, poor-ish neighborhood. It was actually really bad, but I was young, so I couldn't tell." Her mother latched onto to what turned out to be an amazing opportunity, to enroll her daughter in KIPP Gaston, which landed Jackson in a prestigious college. Make no mistake. KIPP Gaston does a great job, but it's no Horace Mann. There's no mixing with elite white and Asian students from big cities, which can bring more social exposure and other opportunities. Jackson arrived at F&M feeling intimidated and lonely. And also without a winter coat – a must-have in snowy Lancaster. Slowly, she withdrew, not asking for help. As a result, her first semester there was awful. She didn't flunk out, but it was close. And she doubted that she belonged. The lack of a winter coat wasn't the only problem, but it was a factor. It's not clear that colleges get the difference between people such as Donnell Butler and Mya Jackson. They require very different levels of assistance, very different approaches to make them feel comfortable, and welcome, on campuses.

Make micro-grants for needy college students commonplace

If there were an easy solution to deep poverty, we would have found it during President Lyndon B. Johnson's war on poverty. Let's set that aside for a moment and focus, instead, on Mya Jackson's coat, described above. To understand the full breadth of this problem, you have to multiply her missing coat by a thousand. There are sudden medical bills, unexpected trips home to deal with family setbacks, the realization that attending the freshman orientation is required, not optional, and you have no way to buy plane tickets. The bottom line: Even the most generous scholarships don't cover everything.[23]

The solution? Personal micro-grants can have a huge positive impact there. Most promising is the possibility of personalizing philanthropy. To have an impact here, your last name doesn't have to be Gates or Zuckerberg. Just pick out one high school you know something about and trust the staff, and sign on for micro-grants. It would be a $500 grant for a trip home for a family emergency, a $1,000 short-term loan until the next housing allowance arrives, $300 for books, $400 for food.

In 2017, KIPP sent out a survey to 10,000 former students, netting 2,969 responses from KIPPsters in college. The most shocking finding: 43 percent said they had missed meals so they could have money for books, fees, and other expenses. Most ominous: 57 percent worried that food would run out before more money for food arrived. "Forty percent of our kids skip meals. Skip meals!" said KIPP CEO Richard Barth. "For people who are real believers in the work we do, that's a wake-up call. Let's figure out how to solve that."

At KIPP Gaston, there are two ways they address these funding gap problems. They found a donor who lives in Durham and is willing to make targeted grants. One type of grant helps students who are admitted to a selective college that is slightly more expensive than a less selective college (one from which they are less likely to earn a degree). The donor steps in to make up the difference.

At times, Amar, the [former] school leader at KIPP Gaston High School, and other staff members come up with personal donations. Amar recalls when Jackson came back from Franklin & Marshall after her first semester and stopped by her old high school to volunteer. "She was miserable," said Amar. "We started talking, and a million things came out about why she was miserable." One reason: the lack of a winter coat kept her from walking across campus to see friends. "So I ordered her some winter gear and I gave her one of my old coats."

When I met with Jackson at F&M, she was wearing the long underwear Amar had ordered, as well as the coat. And things were picking up academically. She was connecting to fellow students and on-campus advisers and staying in touch with Amar and other former KIPP teachers. "This semester is actually like a complete 360," she told me. Here's one insight into how F&M started tracking her more closely: When I interviewed then-President Dan Porterfield, he knew exactly who she was, the difficulties she experienced the first semester, and how things were turned around.

Instead of the patchwork system out there now to help first-generation students through tough spots, what's needed are small grants, said Amar. "It's amazing to me, and I don't think I had a good perspective on this until our kids started going to college, how $1,000 can stand in your way. It's frustrating. If we had a really good micro-grant system, that would actually solve many of our college persistence problems." In December 2018, KIPP announced it was expanding its micro-grant programs – emergency cash to boost college persistence – to four more KIPP regions.[24]

For an example of what's possible here, look to the Panther Retention Grants at Georgia State University, emergency funding for unforeseen and everyday expenses to keep students enrolled. In 2017, roughly 2,000 students received those grants, many of them as little as $300. That grant program is one reason the college success rate there for underrepresented students has risen 23 percentage points since 2002.[25]

Trim back dubious merit aid

Colleges that see themselves in a fight for academically talented students coming from well-off families use merit aid – the offer of scholarship money to convince students and parents they are getting a discount – to win that battle.[26] From the perspective of the colleges, it works. Drawing in top-scoring students from middle- and high-income families allows them to look good on college rankings and maintain costly academic offerings while also offering some need-based scholarships to low-income students. But deep down, they have to recognize it's a shell game that doesn't have to be played. The pioneer here, again, is Dan Porterfield, who just stepped down as president of Franklin & Marshall College to take over leadership at the Aspen Institute. Porterfield eliminated merit aid at F&M. "Money spent on price discounting, on merit aid, wasn't leading to attracting strong students," he said. "Good students, yes, but not near as economically diverse and inclusive as we could be, and as a result, the talent pool wasn't as deep as it could be. The shift to need-based aid was a good thing."

Handing out merit aid is just another reminder that colleges and universities could be doing a lot more for low-income students, especially the most talented. Roughly 86,000 more low-income students a year could be attending top universities, those with the highest college success rates, estimates the Georgetown University Center for Education and the Workforce, given that their standardized test scores were the equal of those who were admitted.[27] The sad irony here: It often costs low-income students more money to attend those less-competitive colleges.[28]

Resist college success strategies that exclude students or lower standards

It's possible to bring about quick change in education; look at what happened with rising high school graduation rates. Over the past decade, district superintendents drove high school completion rates into the mid-80 percent range. Was that truly progress? Some, perhaps, but the big drivers appear to be from factors such as eliminating exit exams and offering weaker alternative diplomas. "A high school diploma today means a lot less than it used to," said Rick Hess, director of education policy studies at the American Enterprise Institute, who has been studying the college completion dilemma.[29] The same "disease" could break out in higher education if, for example, well-meaning state legislators get careless in changing funding formulas to reward colleges for achieving high graduation rates. It's called performance-based funding, and many states are headed down that path.[30] Sounds logical, and could be promising if done right, but just as high school principals knew all the tricks to drive up graduation rates without improving actual learning, college presidents know how to game the system on their end as well.

There are two equally unsavory options. The first: Admit fewer students who are less prepared and at greater risk of not graduating. Problem is, that shrinks the number of first-generation students winning degrees. The second: Degrade the value of a college degree, just as high school principals did by making it easier to graduate. That would boost the number of degrees handed out but diminish the market value of the degrees. "We need to be really thoughtful about heavy-handed fixing and policy solutions that distort incentives," said Hess. He's right. Either of those two bad options could trigger setbacks to the breakthrough.

Colleges must take on the tracking role

The charter networks, KIPP especially, invented the college tracking system, in which counselors using specially adapted Salesforce software follow students through college, especially the first two years, making sure no balls get dropped. How effective is that? It's impossible to separate the college tracking from other college success strategies, such as revamping K-12 classes to make students into more independent learners or using powerful software programs to match each student to the college most likely to ensure they will graduate. My sense, and it's only a gut instinct from interviewing, is that college tracking is the weakest of the links – and the most expensive. KIPP spends $2,000 per student per year for its New York alumni. As class sizes swell in the coming years, there's no way that can be sustained at the same level. Can colleges take over that role? Most of the elite colleges and universities already take this on, but most first-generation students are in barely selective universities that do far less.

Counseling first-generation students at non-selective universities is especially important because those are places where courses required for a major are most likely to fill up fast. At Princeton, the university president is likely to hear from the parents of any student who doesn't get into Econ 101. But, of course, Princeton has the resources to ensure that rarely happens. At the non-selective universities, however, failing to get into an introductory class that's necessary to pursue that major is a common problem. In past years, when California was starving its public universities, that issue was one of the reasons why the college success rates at the big California charter networks lagged behind those of their East Coast counterparts.[31] Getting forced off a graduation path means college just got a lot more expensive, and that's something these students can't absorb.

"At a big open-access school, when the classes for Accounting 101 get full, then you're stuck taking courses that don't you put on track to a major, and you're delayed a semester, and all of a sudden, you fall off," said Sarah Turner, the higher education researcher who has focused on first-generation college-goers. Good counseling, such as passing along insider's knowledge about how to land a seat in the crucial class, can make a huge difference.

Turner is skeptical that the tool both charter networks and universities are pursuing, sophisticated text messaging designed to keep students on track, will suffice. "I don't think that just sending students text messages to renew their FAFSA is going to move the dial much. My guess is that if you didn't renew your FAFSA, there's something else going on. It could be your car broke down and you haven't gotten to school. You've missed a bunch of classes, and now you're so far behind and you don't know what you're going to do. For kids who are disadvantaged, everything unravels more quickly."

LESSON: THE PERSONAL TOUCH WILL REMAIN NECESSARY.

It was the personal touch, at KIPP Gaston, educators who daily told the students they were college material, that propelled so many of their alumni into and through college, with 63 percent earning a bachelor's degree. For the Gaston alumni, that was a breakthrough. Ashley Copeland put it best: If not for KIPP Gaston, "I wouldn't be talking to you." She's right.

ACKNOWLEDGMENTS

Roughly two years ago, after finishing *The Founders,*

a book on the early charter school pioneers, I was in a position to take on something new. Naturally, I asked others for their advice: What's an education issue meriting a book that hasn't been done? KIPP CEO Richard Barth didn't hesitate: College success for first-generation students. Not just getting them into college, but through. Immediately, I knew he was right.

My first take on that was The Alumni series, which looked at what the top charter organizations had discovered while trying to fulfill the college success vows they had made to parents years earlier. The Alumni led to *The B.A. Breakthrough*, a broader look at the efforts to raise college success rates for low-income minority students. There really is a breakthrough afoot, so I owe thanks to Barth for that original suggestion.

I am also indebted to The 74 co-founder Romy Drucker, who has shepherded *The Founders*, The Alumni, and now *The B.A. Breakthrough*, from ideation through publication. *The Founders* started as a magazine-length piece and, over many months, morphed into a book, all with Romy's encouragement. "Why don't you just write another few thousand words; we'll see where that takes us." It revealed a lot about her vision. Kathy Moore, executive editor at The 74, and copy editor Joseph McCombs put in meticulous editing efforts, The 74's senior editor for special projects Emmeline Zhao and its video director Jim Fields brought the book to life on camera. Designers Avec and developers Devona made the online experience of this story beautiful and engaging.

My readers, Josh Wyner from the Aspen Institute; former Vassar College president Catharine Bond Hill, now with Ithaka S+R; Sandy Baum from the Urban Institute; and longtime former KIPP communications director Steve Mancini, helped keep me on the right path. Many excesses got dropped to the cutting room floor; many omissions got added. But please, don't hold them accountable for my views. Both Wyner and Aspen President Dan Porterfield helped me shape the content on the higher education side, not my usual reporting area. Wyner insisted I go see the community college summer program at UCLA. I balked [it was at a time when I was supposed to be writing, not traveling], but I went, and it was well worth seeing. Porterfield has extraordinary thematic vision – the reason he was chosen to lead Aspen, I assume. And, of course, thanks to Dan for writing the preface. Again, he paints a picture I can't presume to paint.

I owe thanks to the founders at KIPP Gaston, Tammi Sutton and Caleb Dolan, who graciously shared their histories, and the same thanks to the KIPP Gaston founding Class of 2009. I'm sure they puzzled on their private Facebook page and in conversations with one another about sharing their personal stories with an unknown gray-haired writer, but they generously did.

Without the generosity of the Walton Family Foundation, I would not have been able to research either The Alumni or *The B.A. Breakthrough*. And without the generosity of the Bill & Melinda Gates Foundation, CityBridge Foundation, the George W. Brackenridge Foundation and others, I would not have been able to turn that research into a book.

If not for the transcription talents of Lindsay Brown, this book would have come out at least a year later. Unfortunately, I've probably forever lost her to a "real" job as a lawyer, which is why this may be my last book.

And finally, a special thanks to my wife, Robin Gradison, who tolerated what she insists should be my last book. No more disappearing into books! Probably good advice.

Richard Whitmire

ENDNOTES

Introduction

1. Camera, Laura. "NAEP Shows Little to No Gains in Math and Reading for U.S. Students." *U.S. News and World Report.* April 10, 2018.

2. Jaschik, Scott. "ACT Scores Drop." *Inside Higher Ed.* October 22, 2018.

3. "Indicators of Higher Education Equity in the United States." Pell Institute, 2018.

4. Aldeman, Chad. "College Dropouts Now Exceed High School Dropouts. What Are We Going to Do About it?" *Education Reform Now.* April 25, 2018.

5. Leonhardt, David. "The Growing College Graduation Gap." *The New York Times.* March 25, 2018.

6. Jaschik, Scott. "The Missing Students." *Inside Higher Education.* December 11, 2012.

7. "What is the Excellence Gap?" Jack Kent Cooke Foundation.

8. Wermund, Benjamin. "U.S. News revamps formula for its latest college rankings." *Politico.* September 10, 2018.

9. Wermund, Benjamin. "How U.S. News college rankings promote economic inequality on campus." *Politico.* September 10, 2017.

10. "Term Enrollment Estimates Current Spring." National Student Clearinghouse Research Center. 2018.

11. "Policy Perspectives." The Educational Policy Institute. February, 2013.

12. "Pursuing the American Dream: Economic Mobility Across Generations." Pew Charitable Trust. July, 2012.

13. Ibid.

Chapter 1

1. Kopp, Wendy. *One Day, All Children...: The Unlikely Triumph of Teach for America and What I learned Along the Way.* PublicAffairs. April, 2001.

Chapter 2

1. "The Condition of Education: Immediate College Enrollment Rate." National Center for Education Statistics. January, 2018.

2. "Indicators of Higher Education Equity in the United States." Pell Institute. 2018 Historical Trend Report.

3. Hess, Frederick and Erickson, Lanae. "Elevating College Completion." American Enterprise Institute. June, 2018.

4. Leonhardt, David. "The Growing College Graduation Gap." *The New York Times.* March 25, 2018.

5. "Signature Report." National Student Clearinghouse Research Center. February, 2018.

6. Nichols, Andrew. "A Look at Latino Student Success." The Education Trust. December 14, 2017.

7. Nichols, Andrew and Evans-Bell, Denzel. "A Look at Black Student Success." The Education Trust. March 1, 2017.

8. Nichols, Andrew. "7 Key Takeaways on Degree Attainment for Black Adults." The Education Trust. August, 2018.

9. Nichols, Andrew and Eberle-Sudre, Kimberlee and Welch, Meredith. "Rising Tide II: Do Black Students Benefit as Grad Rates Increase?" The Education Trust. March 22, 2016.

10. Vandal, Bruce. "Remedial Education's Role in Perpetuating Achievement Gaps." Complete College America. February 12, 2016.

11. Nichols, Andrew. "The Pell Partnership: Ensuring a Shared Responsibility for Low-Income Student Success." The Education Trust. September 24, 2015.

12. Fries, Melissa. "Up to 20 Percent of High School Students Plan to Go to College but Don't Show Up. How Parents, Counselors, and Schools Can Help Stop Summer Melt. *The 74.* July 9, 2018.

13. Backstrand, Jeffrey and Donaldson, Kristi. "Post-Secondary Outcomes of Newark High School Graduates." Newark City of Learning Collaborative. July, 2018.

14. Wall, Patrick. "More Newark students are going to college, but only one in four earns degree within six years, new report finds. *Chalkbeat.* July 30, 2018.

15. Petrilli, Michael. "Not just college: Technical education as a pathway to the middle class." Brookings Social Mobility Memos. April 1, 2016.

16. Barth, Richard. "The Debate About College Shouldn't Be A Debate At All." *Forbes.* June 28, 2018.

17. Whitmire, Richard. *Why Boys Fail: Saving Our Sons from an Educational System That's Leaving Them Behind.* Amacom. 2010.

18. "First-Generation College Survey." Students for Education Reform. 2017.

Chapter 3

1. Fuller, Joseph and Raman, Manjari. "Dismissed by Degrees." Harvard Business School. 2017.

2. Hess, Frederick and Addison, Grant. "A Blow Struck Against the College Cartel." *National Review.* September. 4, 2018.

3. Koran, Mario. "More Than Half of California's High School Grads Still Don't Meet Minimum Requirements for the State's Own Public Universities. *The 74.* August 1, 2018.

4. "Within Our Reach." New York Equity Coalition. May, 2018.

5. "KIPP Announces Findings From its First-Ever Survey of KIPP Alumni in College." January 31, 2017.

6. "Learning While Earning." Georgetown University Center on Education and the Workforce. 2015.

7. Griffin, Riley. "U.S. Students Spend More Time Working Paid Jobs Than Going to Class." *Bloomberg.* September 20, 2018.

8. "What is the Excellence Gap?" Jack Kent Cooke Foundation.

Chapter 4

1. Chingos, Matthew. "What matters most for college completion? Academic preparation is a key predictor of success." American Enterprise Institute. May 30, 2018.

Chapter 5

1. Whitmire, Richard. *The Founders: Inside the revolution to invent (and reinvent) America's best charter schools. The 74.* 2016.

2. Whitmire, Richard. *The 74.* 2017.

Chapter 6

1. Heath, Chip and Heath, Dan. Simon & Schuster. 2017.

2. Toppo, Greg. "HBCUs Doing Something Right for KIPP Alumni." *Inside Higher Ed.* April 5, 2018.

Chapter 7

1. Hoxby, Caroline and Turner, Sarah. "Expanding College Opportunities for High-Achieving, Low-Income Students." Stanford Institute for Economic Policy Research. 2013.

2. Ellis, Lindsay. "Many HISD students aren't making it to college — let alone getting a degree." *Houston Chronicle.* April 16, 2018.

Chapter 9

1. "The Transfer Maze: The High Cost to Students and the State of California."

2. Kolodner, Meredith and Racino, Brad and Quester, Brandon. "The community college segregation machine. Too many black and Latino students get stuck in remedial classes, thwarting college dreams." *The Hechinger Report.* December 13, 2017.

3. Hotchkiss, Michael. "Princeton offers admission to 13 students in reinstated transfer program." Office of Communications, Princeton University.

4. Menchaca, Megan. "UT-Austin's four-year graduation rate reaches all-time high, despite failing 2012 goal." *The Daily Texan.* September 28, 2018.

Chapter 10

1. "Informing Students about Their College Options: A Proposal for Expanding College Opportunities Project." The Hamilton Project. June, 2013.

Conclusion

1. Barshay, Jill. "Federal data shows 3.9 million students dropped out of college with debt in 2015 and 2016." *The Hechinger Report.* November 6, 2017.

2. Whitmire, Richard. "Are High Schools Adequately Preparing Teens for College? No One Really Knows. That's Why Today's GreatSchools Analysis Is One of the Most Important Education Reports in Years." *The 74.* April 25, 2018.

3. Disare, Monica. "How one Manhattan district has preserved its own set of elite high schools." *Chalkbeat.* June 7, 2018.

4. Whitmire, Richard. "'It's Heartbreaking': Boston Parents Ask Why Their Wealthy Neighbors Are Fighting Charter Schools." *The 74.* October 4, 2016.

5. Matos, Alejandro and Webb, Shelby. "Study: Texas students don't gain much by taking college courses in high school." *Houston Chronicle.* July 27, 2018.

6. Meltzer, Erica. 'What are we supposed to feel here?' Education reformers look for answers amid a blue wave." *Chalkbeat.* November 28, 2018.

7. *Reinventing America's Schools: Creating a 21st Century Education System.* Bloomsbury USA. 2017.

8. Backstrand, Jeffrey and Donaldson, Kristi. "Post-Secondary Outcomes of Newark High School Graduates." Newark City of Learning Collaborative. July, 2018.

9. Pondiscio, Robert. "In New York City, Charter Schools are Accomplishing Something Exam Schools Aren't." *EducationNext.* June 15, 2018.

10. Whaley, Monte. "Many Colorado high schools fail to get grads to top tier colleges." *The Denver Post.* December 20, 2018.

11. Phenicie, Carolyn. "Gates Foundation Announces $92 Million Going to School Networks Working to Boost High School Graduation, College Enrollment." *The 74.* August 28, 2018.

12. Barth, Richard. "A United Front: Districts And Charters Collaborate For College Success." *Forbes.* August 9, 2018.

13. Toppo, Greg. "HBCUs Doing Something Right for KIPP Alumni." *Inside HIgher Ed.* April 5, 2018.

14. Cooper, Preston. "Why Do College Dropouts Fail To Repay Their Student Loans?" *Forbes.* August 9, 2018.

15. Shaw, Jane. "How to Make Elite Colleges Less Elitist." *RealClearEducation.* October 6, 2017.

16. Berman, Jillian. "Public colleges spend $5 billion less per year on students of color." *Barron's.* April 9, 2018.

17. Selingo, Jeffrey. "Why do so many students drop out of college? And what can be done about it?" *The Washington Post.* June 8, 2018.

18. Carey, Kevin. "Why More Colleges Should Treat Students Like Numbers." *Washington Monthly.* September/October 2018.

19. Ibid.

20. Jaquette, Ozan and Salazar, Karina. "Colleges Recruit at Richer, Whiter High Schools." *The New York Times.* April 13, 2018.

21. Marcus, Jon. "Panicked universities in search of students are adding thousands of new majors." *The Hechinger Report.* August 9, 2018.

22. Hough, Lory. "Poor, but Privileged." *Harvard Ed Magazine.* Summer, 2017.

23. Morrissey, Janet. "Even With Scholarships, Students Often Need Extra Financial Help." *The New York Times.* April 5, 2018.

24. Vara-Orta, Francisco. "To help them across the college finish line, alums of KIPP charters in four new cities will be eligible for emergency cash." *Chalkbeat.* December 17, 2018.

25. Zatynski, Mandy. "Georgia State: Leading the Way in Student Success." The Education Trust. July 5, 2016.

26. Korn, Melissa. "Prizes for Everyone: How Colleges Use Scholarships to Lure Students." *The Wall Street Journal.* April 17, 2018.

27. "The 20% Solution." Georgetown Center on Education and the Workforce. May, 2017.

28. Hoxby, Caroline and Turner, Sarah. "Expanding College Opportunities." *EducationNext.* Fall, 2013.

29. Hess, Frederick and Erickson, Lanae. "Elevating College Completion." American Enterprise Institute. June, 2018.

30. (Multiple authors) "Does Performance Funding Work?" *Inside Higher Ed.* October 6, 2016.

31. Whitmire, Richard "California Charter Schools Must Work on College Success Rates." *The Orange County Register.* August. 15, 2017.

INDEX

ABOUT THE AUTHOR

Richard Whitmire, a veteran newspaper reporter, is a former editorial writer at USA Today. He is the author of *The Founders: Inside the revolution to invent (and reinvent) America's best charter schools; On the Rocketship: How High Performing Charter Schools are Pushing the Envelope* and *The Bee Eater: Michelle Rhee Takes on the Nation's Worst School District*. Whitmire also wrote *Why Boys Fail: Saving Our Sons from an Education System That's Leaving Them Behind* and co-authored *The Achievable Dream: College Board Lessons on Creating Great Schools*.

THE 74

ABOUT THE 74

The 74 (the74million.org) is a nonprofit media organization dedicated to ensuring that education issues remain front-page headlines every day – to underscoring the broader stakes for our children (and our nation) in improving America's school system.

Since its debut in 2015, The 74 has been on the front lines in covering every key education issue impacting students, families and school leaders across the country, setting the tone in the daily conversation about what's important for tens of millions of kids in our nation's classrooms. Known for both its breadth and depth of coverage, The 74 has distinguished itself with award-winning video and longform journalism, its digital and public engagement, and its partnerships with established outlets.

The B.A. Breakthrough is the second book published by The 74. The first, 2016's *The Founders*, also written by Richard Whitmire, received widespread praise from educators, experts and school leaders across the country. The 74 also collaborated with author David Osborne on the highly acclaimed *Reinventing America's Schools: Creating a 21st Century Education System*.

Sign up to receive daily headlines, analysis and insights at The74Million.org/Newsletter, and go deeper inside *The B.A. Breakthrough* at The74Million.org/Breakthrough.